**DON'T LET THIS
HAPPEN TO YOU!
READ THIS BOOK.**

ADVERTISING IN THE YELLOW PAGES

How to Boost Profits and Avoid Pitfalls

by

W. F. Wagner

HARVEST PRESS, LOS ANGELES, CALIFORNIA

ADVERTISING IN THE YELLOW PAGES

How To Boost Profits and Avoid Pitfalls

by W. F. Wagner

Published by:

Harvest Press
15237 Sunset Boulevard
Los Angeles, CA 90272
(213) 459-3824

ISBN 0-940969-00-9
Library of Congress Catalog Card number 86-83085

Library of Congress Cataloging-in-Publication Data

Wagner, W. F., 1944-
    Advertising in the yellow pages.

    Includes index.
    1. Advertising. 2. Telephone--Directories--Yellow pages. 3. Advertising layout and typography. I. Title
HF6146.T4W34 1986   659.13'2   86-83085
ISBN 0-940969-00-9 (pbk.)

Preface

W. F. Wagner is a former teacher who became a Yellow Pages salesperson for one reason: Money. Within two years in Yellow Pages sales, his annual income was among the top one percent in the nation. He was promoted to Director of Training, and then to Sales Manager, to train and manage other salespeople for the same financial success.

In this book, Wagner shares with you industry secrets he has learned. He answers all your questions about the Yellow Pages and offers you inside information you are unlikely to get elsewhere.

W. F. Wagner is a pseudonym used to protect relatives, friends and acquaintances still connected with the Yellow Pages industry.

Acknowledgements

Thanks to R. Mitchell for her many excellent editorial suggestions.

Thanks to D. A. Morris, my esteemed colleague at the Yellow Pages, for reading this manuscript and making many insightful contributions.

Thanks to H. S. Klinvex for giving generously of her time and quick mind.

Thanks to Art Wand for his magical tips.

Thanks to Alex for his masterful cartoons.

And a particular thanks to my spouse for loads of miscellaneous help and particularly for resisting the temptation to take a meat cleaver to my skull when I was being unpleasant to live with during the sometimes frustrating process of writing this book.

Table of Contents

Chapter Three
WHAT YOU NEED TO KNOW
ABOUT YOUR OWN BUSINESS..................95

Chapter One

WHY
YOU NEED
THIS BOOK

When **Bill Dugan** of T-Tops Unlimited was visited by a salesperson from the Yellow Pages, he refused to renew his advertising. Bill insisted that during the year he had asked everyone who called or came into his store how they had found him, and not one had said "The Yellow Pages."

Bill specializes in selling and installing T-Tops, a type of hard convertible piece that fits in the roofs of some sports cars. Because T-Tops are a frequent target of burglars, selling them can be very lucrative. Bill makes a hefty profit of $300 a pair.

The year before, when he was contacted by a representative of the Yellow Pages, it seemed a good idea to advertise. Unfortunately, there was no heading for T-Tops, so Bill's ad was put under the heading "Automobile Sun Roofs." The problem was that when shoppers needing a T-Top looked it up, they found no such heading. Their next likely stop, the Index, listed T-Tops. But since there was no such heading, people were referred to three related ones, none of which was "Automobile Sun Roofs." The result was a total loss of Bill's investment in the Yellow Pages for the previous year.

Unfortunately, Bill didn't know that the salesperson who arranged his ad had only been on the job for a week and didn't realize she was putting Bill's ad at a heading where no one would look for it.

Jimmy Nelson, whose business consists of repairing and replacing brakes, complained that all day long his work was interrupted by telephone calls from shoppers who wanted estimates. Since he used superior materials and hired more skilled workers than his competitors did, naturally his prices were higher. As a result, he got many telephone calls, but not many jobs. His Yellow Pages ad was costing him precious time and not even producing enough business to pay for itself, let alone to make him a profit.

Jimmy had been pretty busy when his salesperson dropped in on him the year before, so he had let her put his ad together. Unfortunately, she had not asked Jimmy much about his business and the kinds of customers he wanted to reach. As a result, Jimmy's ad invited calls for estimates in large, bold letters, but nowhere mentioned the high quality of his work.

Clara Able, the owner of Ames Plumbing, claimed she hadn't gotten any business from the Yellow Pages. Her ad was one of four large Display ads on the first page of the Plumbing Contractors heading, but a single glance at it in the context of the other three explained her poor results.

It was flat, employing none of the standout techniques used in the other three ads. The plumbers who shared the page with Clara said they were satisfied with their results, but she lost a year's good business and profitable return on the money she invested.

How had this happened? Clara's salesperson was in a hurry the year before and didn't have time to make the few changes in Clara's ad that would have made it an eye stopper.

Artie Hoffman spent five times what he should have to advertise his welding operation because his salesperson was after a big commission, and Artie didn't know any better.

Sue Violet, a florist, bought unnecessary advertising in directories outside her local area because her salesperson lied and said her main competitor was doing it.

The ad for **Shine Builders** was put under the heading "Contractors-Building, General" because the salesperson was inexperienced and didn't know that "Contractors-Alteration" was the heading that got most of the lookups. They lost a potential bundle.

None of this would have happened if these advertisers had this book. Instead, not knowing enough about the Yellow Pages to put together an effective program, they relied on the say so of Yellow Pages salespeople—with disastrous results.

THE BUSINESS OWNER'S DILEMMA

Each year you and other business owners spend billions of dollars to advertise in the Yellow Pages. It's not surprising. The Yellow Pages have a reputation for working. Almost every - body is familiar with the Yellow Pages, which receives millions of lookups everyday by consumers who are ready to buy.

Everywhere you go you'll find Yellow Pages directories full of ads representing all kinds of businesses. The owners of these businesses aren't advertising because they plan to lose money. On the contrary, advertisers in the Yellow Pages can expect to get more mileage per dollar spent there than from investments in any other advertising medium.

Yet, casualties of this billion dollar industry, like those described above, are all too common. In most cases, the bulk of the dollars invested by advertisers in the Yellow Pages might better be spent at the crap tables—the gamble wouldn't be any bigger, and at least they'd have some fun!

As it is, most of you probably take the hit-and-miss approach, guessing at which directories to advertise in, what headings to list under, what ad sizes to buy, and what should go in your ads. Or worse, you leave those decisions up to Yellow Pages salespeople. The result is that your hopes and expectations of profiting aren't met.

This situation borders on tragedy. The Yellow Pages are indeed rich in gold, but few of you know how to mine it!

THE TWO TYPES OF ADVERTISING

You may not be aware of this, but there are only two types of advertising. One is "creative" and includes television, radio, magazines, newspapers, billboards, and direct mail. You advertise in these media to reach out to potential customers and create a desire in them to buy what you sell. Someone who has been having thoughts of redecorating her living room may become interested in buying your carpeting or furniture when she opens the newspaper and notices the attractive prices you are offering during your spring sale.

CREATIVE MEDIA
Creates a Desire to Buy

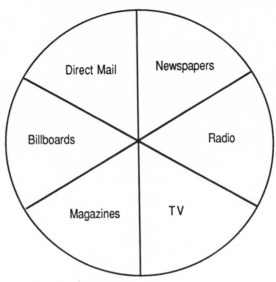

DIRECTIVE MEDIA
Directs a Buyer to You

Creative advertising media may stimulate a desire in a consumer to buy, but the purchase may not occur right then. The prospective buyer may not hear your message or for various reasons may not respond right away. Thus, creative media deliver your advertising message randomly, and not necessarily when the prospect is ready to act upon hearing it.

The prospect may have no immediate need for your product or urgent desire to buy it. He may want to check your competitors or take a look at other brands. Being short on funds may stop him from making the purchase immediately. Or the tendency to procrastinate can delay a sale.

To make matters worse, statistics from tests conducted at Northwestern University indicate that a day after consumers are exposed to your ad, 25 percent have forgotten who you are. Two days' passing result in 50 percent not remembering. And after a week, 97 percent will not recall you. (Ironically, they may still be left with the desire to buy!)

The second type of advertising is "directive" because it directs the buyer to a seller when he is ready to buy. **Aside from the classifieds in the newspaper, the Yellow Pages is the only directive advertising medium.**

When you are spending money on creative advertising, you must also use directive advertising to protect the dollars you spend creating desire in people to buy your product or service. When customers are ready to buy, they are most likely to turn to the Yellow Pages because it has a year-long life. If they can find you, chances are they will do business with you. If not, your competitor will benefit from your past investment in creative advertising.

Here's how the two kinds of advertising work together. For years Mrs. Summers has been seeing your newspaper ads or hearing your radio commercials in which you offer the widest selection of name brand televisions at discount prices. You have successfully created an interest in her buying a television from you. Now she needs a new television. With your name vaguely in mind, she goes to the Yellow Pages and finds your ad, or sees your listing under the brand name she wants to buy. The name immediately clicks, and she calls your number. You've made a sale.

THE MOST EFFECTIVE WAY TO ADVERTISE

The combination of creative media with Yellow Pages has proven to be the most effective way to advertise. Yellow Pages do not compete with, but complement other types of advertising. Other forms of advertising don't reduce the need for Yellow Pages advertising—they *increase* it. You want to protect the dollars you spend on creative advertising.

Creative media typically have a short lifespan. Chances are that when a person is ready to buy, he will not have the newspaper in which your ad ran or turn on the radio in hopes of catching your commercial. But he *is* likely to have a copy of the Yellow Pages around and look you up to get your address or telephone number or refresh his memory of your name.

If you are not visible there, the hard-earned dollars you spent creating his desire for your product or service will go to benefit one of your competitors. When your prospect is finally in a buying frame of mind, the Yellow Pages are right there. Unlike the newspaper, radio commercial, or billboard, the Yellow Pages book is geared to *active* shoppers, who are your best bet for a sale.

WHY THE YELLOW PAGES?

Aside from being accessible and easy to use, there is a compelling reason for the Yellow Pages. Think about this.

A business that has been around for a while has a customer base. The average business, however, loses approximately 10 percent of its customers each year, usually through no fault of its own. Carrying a yearly 10 percent loss of customers to its logical conclusion, the average business can expect to experience a complete turnover of customers every ten years!

Customers move. They satisfy their needs (they buy an automobile) and are unlikely to make a similar purchase soon. Sometimes a customer doesn't pay his bills, and you decide to drop him. There are also the dissatisfied customers, as in, "No matter how hard you try...."

THE CUSTOMER CIRCUIT

YOUR CUSTOMER BASE
People who have YOU in mind

Referrals	Solicited by your Salespeople	Passed by Your Location	Saw Your Advertising	Former Customers

10% are lost each year — 100% are lost in ten years!
You MUST get new customers

YOUR NEW CUSTOMER POSSIBILITIES
People who have NO ONE in mind

Comparison Shoppers	Buyers of Infrequently Purchased Items	Newcomers to the Area	Your Competition's Unhappy Customers	Emergency Buyers

These are BIG Yellow Pages Users
75% will continue to deal with you once they start

FACT #1. *A business must get new customers regularly if it is to continue to operate at its current level, not to mention experience growth.* Where do these customers come from? Some of your potential new customers start out looking specifically for you. This includes referrals—people who are sent your way by other customers. There are new accounts solicited by your salespeople in the field. If your location is attractive, passers-by are bound to account for a share of your new customers. Advertising special sales will also generate new customers.

FACT #2. *Of the buyers who start out looking specifically for you, almost one-half may end up doing business with another firm because (1) they cannot find you, or (2) they succumb to a competitor's advertising if it is more visible or persuasive or contains more information.*

Other potential new customers don't have someone they are in the habit of doing business with. This group includes comparison shoppers who may want to check prices of a product or service with several different suppliers. It also includes buyers of a product or service purchased infrequently (such as a new roof or an automobile). Newcomers or visitors to the area, or people buying a product or service for the first time, also belong to this group. Your competitor's dissatisfied customers, who did not like his service or prices, may now be looking for a new company to deal with. There are also the emergency buyers who need something on the double, such as a water pipe repair job.

This group of potential new customers uses the Yellow Pages more than any other since they do not have a particular business in mind and must search for one.

FACT #3. *Three out of four new customers will continue to do business with you once they have started.* **Let this sink in!** It underlines the importance of being the first to do business with people who make up this group.

Of course, buyers who already know you and who are looking specifically for you will also use the Yellow Pages to get additional facts about you. They may know your name, but need your address or telephone number. They may have only partial recall of your name and need a memory jogger. But if you're not there, they'll call your competitor who is advertising under the same or a similar heading.

Thus, the Yellow Pages fulfill a crucial function for you.

HOW CRITICAL ARE THE YELLOW PAGES TO YOUR BUSINESS?

You have seen that the average business can count on losing approximately 10 percent of its customers each year. You have also seen that the Yellow Pages can help you replace them and keep your business growing. The question is how critical it is for *you* to invest heavily in the Yellow Pages.

If you are not asking your new customers how they heard about you, start doing it now. Ask, because customers don't usually volunteer this information. How many referrals are you getting? How often do you advertise sales in the newspaper, on the radio, or by direct mail? How many customers does that bring you?

Do you have salespeople soliciting customers for you? If so, how well do they do? Does your location bring in many walkers-by? And how loyal are your former customers? The number one reason people chose to deal with a particular business is because they like the people that represent it. In this case, they may go out of their way to deal with a business even if the location is a bit inconvenient or the prices somewhat higher than the competition's. Does this apply to you?

Take a long look at your current customer base and assess its strength. This will tell you how much you must depend upon advertising in the Yellow Pages to reach out for potential new customers who will not come to you through other means.

WHY THERE HAS BEEN NO HELP?

Despite the mega-dollars pulled in each year by the Yellow Pages industry, if you advertise your business and know little about Yellow Pages advertising, you are on your own.

•There is no literature to help you in making Yellow Pages advertising decisions.

•Your fellow advertisers can't help you because they are adrift in the same murky waters as you are.

•Yellow Pages salespeople usually work solely on commission and are extremely pressured to make a sale. Their advice rests on this urgency and is often less than truthful or in your best interests. Time, salespeople's most valuable commodity, simply does not allow them to act as your consultants, despite what they or their company's literature may tell you. Your needs will simply not take precedence over theirs. What's more, the rapid turnover in the industry means that many of its salespeople are too new to know how to make their product work. If for no other reason than this, you need a more reliable and objective source of information on which to base decisions about your investment in the Yellow Pages.

•Advertising agencies? They make their money from commissions paid to them by the media in which they place your ads. In some cases, they bill you additional fees. The more you advertise, the more they make—either through commissions from the media or from your fees. They can hardly be unbiased in their recommendations. The worst of it is that in most cases they probably know little more about the Yellow Pages than you do.

•"Cut and Save" agencies are springing up in response to increased customer confusion over the explosion of Yellow Pages directories. They make commissions on what you spend, claiming to whittle away at the fat in your program, and then take a percentage of what they save you. Because these agencies are generally staffed by former Yellows Pages personnel, they usually have the knowledge to help you. The problem, however, is that their advice may also be biased.

For example, what happens if there is no fat to trim? Or if you are under-advertised and should be spending more? Or if your program is a good one, but leaving it intact means no percentage for them? This conflict of interest once again keeps you from getting objective advice.

The ideal solution, of course, is knowledgeable Yellow Pages consultants who work on an hourly basis and make their living without regard for how much you spend or save. If you find one, hang on.

Because you haven't been able to get the right answers, your dollars are ill-spent and your investments often don't pay off. But a profitable advertising program is not difficult to design, and the money to be made from the Yellow Pages is virtually limitless.

HELP IS AT HAND

This book fills the gap between you and potential profits by giving you all the information you need to create a Yellow Pages program that pays off. In the following pages, you will find answers to your questions and solutions to the problems you face when you decide to try the Yellow Pages.

This book is better than free. It will not cost you a dime because, if used properly, it will definitely make money for you. I base this claim on years of experience. If you read this book and refer to it as you plan your Yellow Pages program, you can't help but have a profitable investment.

You will find out:

• which directories work
• cost-effective ways to beat the competition
• how to get your ad read first
• how to bring in your most profitable customers
• how to introduce a new business, product or service
• how to know what headings to advertise under
• when your obligation to pay for your advertising ceases
• why most businesses throw money away in the Yellow Pages
• how Yellow Pages salespeople attempt to trick you
• And thousands of other money-making suggestions and pieces of helpful information.

There are riches in the Yellow Pages, but you must know how to acquire them. Most people who are now in business, or who intend to start a business, plan to be around for a while.

And so will the Yellow Pages. Yellow Pages directories are generally published annually, which means that the crucial decisions you make about your Yellow Pages advertising affect your business for an entire year.

Here is the information you need to make the right decisions. It pays for itself by showing you how to increase your profits from the Yellow Pages and save money at the same time.

HOW TO USE THIS BOOK

In **Chapter One** you've found out why you need this book. Now you'll find out how to go straight to the information you need for your particular situation.

Chapter Two tells you What the Yellow Pages Are, What They Cost, and What They Offer. It gives you the facts about what directory competition is doing to both your customer potential and advertising expenses and which directories are really used. It catalogs and describes the parts of a Yellow Pages directory, including the types of ads available, and compares them in terms of costs and results. It offers step by step procedures for designing an effective ad that will reach the customers you want to target and offers suggestions on how to improve the position of your ads. It also discusses how directory rates are determined, why they vary, and answers the question "Can rates be negotiated?" It reveals which ads work best, how to find out about and take advantage of freebies, promotionals and discount programs, and gives you the facts about directory distribution.

Chapter Three, What You Need To Know About Your Own Business, tells you what you have to find out about your own operation to put together an effective and money-making advertising program. Armed with information from chapter two, you are now able to apply it by analyzing your own special needs. **Using the Wagner Yellow Pages profit formula outlined here, you will learn how to know what your advertising is really costing.** Find out how many customers you need to pay for your ads, how to compare the costs of different advertising media, directories and ads, and how much you should spend each month on Yellow Pages advertising. You will also learn the three cornerstones of a Yellow Pages advertising program—what ad sizes you need, when to advertise in directories outside your local area, and how to decide which headings to advertise under. Also offered is information on which businesses profit most from the Yellow Pages and ways to find out how your own type of business will do. For ongoing advertisers, there is a special checklist to use in updating your program from year to year.

Chapter Four, How to Deal With Salespeople and What to Watch Out For, takes you inside at the Yellow Pages to show you what makes their salespeople tick. You'll find out how you can protect yourself from becoming a victim of the industry, its salespeople or your own mistakes. It gives you the lowdown on tricks of the trade, the truth about surveys and testimonial letters, and uncovers scare tactics salespeople employ to get you to buy and buy right away. It instructs you on how to keep control of the salescall, the question/answer tactic, why it's a waste of time to play the objection/solution game with salespeople, and special objections you can use to get rid of salespeople—temporarily or permanently. Important information on how to read a contract, how to get an adjustment if an error is made, what you must have in your hands before your salesperson leaves, and how to change your program after you order it is revealed. You are told what to do if you sell or move your business or go out of business altogether. Finally, there are special warnings to both new and continuing advertisers.

Chapter Five, Checking Up on How Your Advertising is Working, tells you how to check results after your advertising is in place. It shows you many different methods to monitor your ads to get good data you can use to change your advertising yearly to reflect successes and failures. It describes how to survey both telephone shoppers and walk-in customers and points out which customers will be missed by surveys. It offers step by step troubleshooting procedures to help you find out where your problems lie and how to correct them. Finally, it tells you where the responsibility of the Yellow Pages stops and yours begins.

As you read, illustrations, graphs, charts and worksheets will assist you in applying what you learn to your own business.

To be a winner at Yellow Pages advertising, you must know as much as you can about the Yellow Pages, how to analyze your own needs, how to protect yourself from the Yellow Pages industry and its representatives, how to find out if you're getting your dollar's worth, and what to do about it if you're not.

Some of you may be starting a business or advertising for the first time, so everything presented here about Yellow Pages advertising will be new to you. Absorb every word. Others of you who are well established in business and are more experienced with the Yellow Pages may find some of the information familiar. But now you will begin to see even this familiar information in a new light. In either case, you will be surprised to find out how much you *don't* know about the Yellow Pages and all you can gain from learning and using this information.

GET READY TO MAKE A PROFIT!

Chapter Two

WHAT THE YELLOW PAGES ARE, WHAT THEY COST, AND WHAT THEY OFFER

All Yellow Pages directories get sufficient usage to offer the advertiser an avenue to profit. In a survey, not a single directory failed to produce customers for some businesses.

For this reason, no directory in your marketplace can be eliminated as worthless. Each is potentially profitable. If you know what you're doing, you can afford to have representation in all of them. *The key is to know what you are doing.*

WHERE TO ADVERTISE?

The biggest problem facing Yellow Pages advertisers today is figuring out which directories to advertise in. Gigantic profits have caused intense competition in the Yellow Pages industry. For the consumer, this means they are delivered a number of different Yellow Pages books that look remarkably alike. For you and other advertisers, the effect of the explosion of directories in your marketplaces is frustration and confusion.

When only one Yellow Pages directory covered your marketplace, your job was easier. You simply placed all your advertising there. Since the split up of AT&T and the appearance everywhere of competing directories, your task has become more formidable. Now you have to pick and choose, without reliable information on which to base your choices. You now have to contend with the local telephone company's Yellow Pages directory as well as with competing directories that are also distributed to your customers.

Competing directory companies vie for your advertising dollars by trying to offer you something different or "better."

Sometimes they break up the local directory into smaller areas, resulting in directories called "neighborhoods." Other times the reverse strategy is employed—publishing overlays, combina - tions of two or more telephone company areas into one large directory. This increases the circulation of your ad and theoretically offers you more business potential. Sometimes a competing directory covers the identical area, but at a greatly reduced rate.

Directories can be specialized, geared to minority and special interest groups, such as women, children, Spanish speakers, Blacks or even senior citizens (as in the recent Silver Pages published by Southwestern Bell). Sometimes a specialization revolves around the credibility of its advertisers. The Better Business Bureau directories that include members' ads only fall into this category.

With all the choices, it is no wonder that you are unsure about which directories to advertise in. How did this situation develop?

If five years ago someone had asked you to name the nation's largest publishing company, chances are your guess would have been wrong. But before its breakup as a settlement of an antitrust lawsuit against the telephone conglomerate, AT&T was the largest publishing company in the United States, bringing in 3.5 billion dollars in advertising revenues in 1982 alone.

After the forced divestment breakup, by 1985 the dollars spent by businesses to advertise in the Yellow Pages doubled. The after-tax margins of the Yellow Pages industry are estimated impressively at anywhere from 15 to 35 percent. And everyone wants to grab a piece of the pie.

This very attractive profit potential has caused fierce jockeying for markets by competing independent and telephone affiliated directory companies. All this punching and counter-punching is mild, however, compared to the bouts shaping up today in which the former Bell subsidiaries created by the split-up are fighting one another—jumping across state boundaries to market all sorts of new directories.

Competition existed even in the 1960's when AT&T had a virtual monopoly on Yellow Pages directories, but it was in the form of neighborhood or specialty directories that took too meager a bite of the market to concern the telephone giant.

In the 1970's, large independent telephone companies, such as GTE Corp., began to follow in the footsteps of small, private entrepreneurs and sell ads and distribute their directories in AT&T territory. Recently, large directory publishers not affiliated with the telephone company have begun to compete in several states. (This is in spite of the fact that they sell and publish telephone company directories in others!)

DIRECTORY COMPETITION: HOW YOU SUFFER FROM IT

Today's Yellow Pages situation has been compared to the early days of radio when more than one station began operating in a market. Advertisers screamed because they now had to advertise on more than one station to get the same coverage. But you may have passed up radio advertising because of its high cost. You are more likely to be dependent upon the Yellow Pages to keep your customers flowing in, and so this situation hits harder.

First, there is the obvious confusion about which directories to advertise in. Then, there is the frustration of trying to spread dollars around effectively. There is also the headache of dealing with not one, but with a score of Yellow Pages salespeople. But the biggest headache caused by the increased number of directories in a marketplace is *paying more to reach the same number of customers.*

PAYING MORE FOR THE SAME

To understand, let's look at a typical Yellow Pages advertiser, John Vellachi, a locksmith. Suppose he has 200 people in his marketplace who represent possible customers. If only one Yellow Pages directory is delivered in the area, when a consumer is ready to do business, he has only that one directory to turn to. If John is one of four locksmiths who advertise, all else being equal, he can expect to get 50 customers or 25 percent of the potential business.

Now another directory company invades his turf to compete with the first, and all four locksmiths advertise in both directories. Assuming these directories are equally desirable for the consumer to use, when someone needs a locksmith, he now has a choice of two directories to consult. If of John's 200 potential customers, 100 use the first directory and 100 use the second, he still has only 50 potential customers. In other words, his potential income has not increased by as much as a nickel, but his advertising costs have doubled.

This, in effect, is what the profusion of directories has done: *to reach the same number of customers, you must do more advertising—and at far greater expense. This fact makes this book a necessity for you. If your expenses are higher, your profits must be, too.*

WHICH DIRECTORIES ARE USED?

Most Yellow Pages advertisers like you have no idea how their ads are working. This does not stop them from giving you an opinion, but that is all it is. Once a business owner signs a contract for Yellow Pages advertising, he appears to file the whole subject away with his copy. He doesn't give it another thought until a salesperson walks through the door the following year to renew his program.

It is inconceivable that an auto parts business or a plumbing supply outlet would purchase thousands of dollars worth of parts and then not pay the slightest attention to how they were selling and which were most profitable. And yet this is precisely how most advertisers treat their investment in the Yellow Pages.

Because most businesses do not survey their customers, their opinions about directory usage are usually not worth much. Some don't use the Yellow Pages themselves and make the mistake of assuming that everyone else in the world is like them. (If I thought like that, I would live in a world with no sports - cars, vodka or three piece suits.)

If an advertiser happens to conduct a customer survey, it is usually done in such a haphazard fashion that the results are unreliable. For example, an advertiser might compare how many customers he pulls from a large ad in one directory with how many he gets from a small ad in another directory, totally ignoring the role that different ad sizes play in the picture.

Or he will depend on his customers to tell him which directory they used to find him. Consumers don't usually discriminate between telephone directories. All directories carry the walking fingers logo and look very much alike. Independent directories are often purposefully designed to resemble telephone company directories to make the consumer think he is using the telephone company publication.

A recent study by an independent market research firm found that anywhere from 25 to 47 percent of people who use the Yellow Pages now rely primarily on independently published books. Even though consumers remain ignorant of this, it makes independent publications as potentially profitable for you as the telephone company directories. Your advertising choices are made even more difficult.

The public's lack of knowledge about the many different directory companies, coupled with the look-alike directories, make it hard to find out which directories consumers are really using. You can't rely on what they say because they don't usually discriminate and can't clearly communicate to you which directory they use. You must *learn* how to get the right information from them.

While the vast majority of Yellow Pages advertisers know little about how their advertising is working, some do keep careful and reliable records of their Yellow Pages customers and the dollars these customers spend. On the basis of their surveys, the bottom line about Yellow Pages usage is this: ALL DIRECTORIES ARE USED. This should provide ample motivation for you to learn how to advertise in a way that lets you capitalize on that usage.

THE PARTS OF A YELLOW PAGES DIRECTORY

The Covers. Pick up a copy of the Yellow Pages. On its front cover you will see the walking fingers logo and the publisher's name. You will also find a statement about the general area the directory covers, with a specific listing of most of the cities included. Few people pay attention to this, but it is very important since it is one of the main factors that sets off one directory from another.

The directory's back cover normally has a map showing the area in which the directory is distributed. If the entire area shown does not get delivery, the map will use different colors to show where telephone numbers are listed only compared to the area that receives delivery. You can use this map to find out precisely where your ads will be seen if you advertise in this directory.

The White Pages. At the front of the directory, you will find a white section called the information pages. These pages usually include some combination of the following: emergency numbers for police and fire departments, area code maps, zip code maps, first aid information, long-distance rates, seating patterns of major entertainment arenas, and other such features. Directory companies compete with one another to include features in the information pages that will make a directory more useful to the consumer. A surprising number of consumers never even look at these pages, but instead spend countless hours on the telephone during the year trying to get information contained in them.

Just after this section, you will find other white pages that alphabetically list businesses within the directory boundaries as well as businesses outside this area that purchase listings. The telephone company also includes residential listings in this section as required by law. Independent competitors normally omit residential listings from their white pages. Since they have no access to telephone company records, they have no way to get these residential numbers.

Telephone company salespeople use as a selling tool the fact that their directory has residential listings while competing directories do not. The truth is, however, that these listings are probably not very useful.

About 20 percent of residential telephone numbers are now unlisted and do not appear in the white pages. Of the remaining 80 percent, about one-third of these listings will become obsolete through disconnects or number changes between the time the white pages are prepared for the printer and the directories are delivered to consumers. As the directory continues to age, even more numbers become outdated. Add to all this the fact that most people keep frequently called telephone numbers in a personal phone book, and the value of residential listings in the white pages seems small. Some consumers have even stated a preference for no residential listings, claiming this saves their having to wade through hundreds of them when looking for a business telephone number.

Some directory companies put the white pages listings behind the more frequently consulted classified yellow pages for the convenience of consumers.

The Index. Some directories feature an Index as part of the information pages. This is useful in directing people to a product or service by page number if there is no category for what they want. For example, someone looking for magnetic tape would not find that heading. The Index, however, would direct him to look under another heading, "Data Processing Supplies," to find what he needs. Without an Index, the customer might turn outside the Yellow Pages to find what he wants. In this case, the vendor of magnetic tape might lose that customer without the Index. (See illustration next page.)

The Classified Yellow Pages. Finally there are the yellow pages that classify businesses into categories called headings. Headings are positioned alphabetically and appear in dark, bold type to make them easier to read.

Heading

Limousine Service
Ace Taxi 935-8303

Real Estate — (CONT'D)

25

A QUICK EASY GUIDE
TO USING
THIS DIRECTORY

Tell-Tales and Heading Cross-References. At the top outer corners of each page are tell-tales, similar to those found in dictionaries, to assist a shopper in finding a heading more rapidly. Heading cross-references, which direct a consumer to one or more closely related headings, are also sprinkled throughout the directory to give additional help to shoppers.

Tell-Tales

MANICURING—MAPS M

Heading Cross-Reference

Hauling
See
Machinery Movers & Erectors
Rubbish Hauling
Trucking

Columns on a Page. Each page is divided into anywhere from three to five vertical columns. The number of columns on a page affects both consumers and advertisers because it determines the size of the print. The fewer the columns, the larger the print, making it more readable. It is estimated that 65 percent of people over the age of 35 either wear glasses or need to. If this is true, larger print may increase a directory's usage. Businesses that provide eye-related services should consider how many of their customers might have trouble reading small print and prefer to use a directory with fewer columns.

In addition to type size, ad size is also affected by the number of columns on a page—the more columns, the smaller an ad. In 1981, several directory publishers were sued for price fixing, fraud and breach of contract in a class-action suit seeking over $85 million in damages. Because the companies changed from a four column to a five-column format without telling the businesses who had contracted for space, advertisers ended up with 20 percent less space than they had bargained for. Directory companies, however, were able to add 20 percent more advertising to each page, reducing the number of pages and their costs at the same time.

Since fewer columns mean more pages are required to accommodate advertising, some directory companies deliberately use fewer columns to make their directories thicker. While costs to produce the directory increase, so does their revenue because some advertisers mistakenly believe that a thicker directory is a more successful one. More on that subject later.

TYPES OF YELLOW PAGES ADS

Incolumn Ads. Items of advertising in the column fall alphabetically. In other words, your position under a heading is determined by the first letter of the name of your business. The exception to this rule is a business beginning with the word "The," as in "The Clark Company," because traditionally such businesses are listed as Clark Company, The.

By the Line. Listings are the most basic form of identity in the Yellow Pages. A Listing, which consists of the name, address and telephone number of a business, can be set in regular (light) type or in a more eye-catching bold type. Some directory companies sell bold listings only with a bold number. Other companies give you a choice. If you have an option, don't purchase your telephone number in bold unless you feel like wasting money. (Who tries to find a business by looking down the list of telephone numbers?)

Extra lines under your listings that provide the consumer with more information, a second telephone number, or directions to your place of business are available as well. These can be important, particularly in describing a hard-to-find location or boasting a convenient one. In addition, there are Cross-Reference listings in regular or bold type that can be used if your business name changes and you want people looking under your former name to be referred to your new one. All these listings are also available in the White Pages.

Worth Remembering

Use extra lines to pinpoint a hard-to-find location or to boast a convenient one.

Examples Of Listings

Regular (light) type listing

ABC Electric
 4110 Main Laurelton...660-1033

Bold type listing

ABC ELECTRIC
 4110 Main Laurelton... 660-1033

Bold type listing with bold number

ABC ELECTRIC
 4110 Main Laurelton... **660-1033**

Super Bold white pages listing

ABC ELECTRIC
 4110 Main Laurelton.. **660-1033**

Extra line for more information

ABC ELECTRIC
 Since 1948
 4110 Main Laurelton... 660-1033

Extra line for second number

ABC Electric
 4110 Main Laurelton... 660-1033
 If Busy Call.. 664-9927

Cross-reference listing

Val's Electric
 See ABC Electric

By the Space. In addition to listings which are sold by the line, there are Incolumn ads sold by the space in half-inch increments, usually up to 3 inches. Space ads are set off by a surrounding box. They offer additional promotional value because unlike listings they allow for descriptive text and some artwork, although it is limited. The number of inches determines the number of lines of information you can include. You may vary the print size and use a combination of capital letters and upper/lower case print, although capital letters and bold print are more eye-compelling and should be reserved for emphasis.

In a space ad, the business name is set in bold capital letters and the address and telephone number in a lighter type at the bottom of the ad. Your text goes in between. Beginning with a one and one-half inch space ad and larger, you may use a box in the upper left corner where information to pinpoint your specialty, hours or location can be inserted. This is a particu-larly good item for you if your hours or location—good or poor—is a key factor in your business.

Incolumn Space Ads

CYCLE WORLD
Machining - Fabrication - Welding
Frame & Engine Modifications
High Performance & Racing
102 S Broadway ---------------- 288-8611

1/2 Inch

BOB'S COINS
Buy - Sell - Trade
APPRAISALS & COIN
INVESTMENT SERV.
U.S. & FOREIGN COINS
SILVER BARS
607 E Center ------------ 872-0608

1 Inch

AMERICAN KENNELS
SINCE 1941   DOGS & CATS
• AIR CONDITIONED
• INDIVIDUAL RUNS
DAILY: 8 - NOON &
1:30 TO 5:30
SATURDAY: 8 TILL NOON
815 Main   239-0968

2 Inch with Box

Trade Ads, also in the column and placed alphabetically, are space ads or listings used for brand name identification. They normally feature a service or product, or simply present the logo of your business.

Trademark ads come in two sizes. The smaller, about one inch deep (excluding the space occupied beneath it by your listing), generally has a logo at the right and text at the left. Your name is set in bold capital letters at the top and repeated in your listing at the bottom. Three sides of the ad are outlined. The larger Trademark ad, called a Custom Trademark, is about twice the size, and offers the option of placing a logo at the top left, right or center of the ad.

Trade Ads

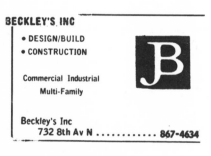

Trademark

Tradename

Custom Trademark

Some Trademark ads are purchased by local businesses. Others are ordered by national companies, and authorized representatives may buy a listing under it. Trademark ads are sometimes offered free or at a nominal charge by directory companies as promotional items, and they are particularly effective if the logo—either yours or that of the national manufacturer—is recognizable.

Directory companies are forever innovative in coming up with new advertising items to sell to you. They recently began to offer Incolumn ads that combine the features of the space ads with those of the the Trademark ad, permitting artwork to be included.

Finally there are Tradename listings which feature the name of a product or service in bold print with the local outlet or representative listed in regular type directly below it.

Display Ads. Open the Yellow Pages to an active heading, such as "Painting Contractors." You will see an abundance of ads, larger than those appearing in the column, that contain illustrations. These are Display ads, sometimes called the ultimate in Yellow Pages advertising. Display ads are purchased by a unit of space. In other words, you buy an amount of space and can put what you want in it, within limits.

Like Incolumn ads, Display ads are purchased in increments. The smallest Display ad is one quarter of a column, and additional quarter column units are joined to form larger ads. This continues until the largest ad offered—sometimes a full page—is reached.

With a Display ad, you must have an Anchor—an Incolumn listing of your business name, address, and telephone number, along with a referral to the page your Display Ad is on. This is so that consumers who look for you in the column are directed to your Display ad for more information. A regular (light) type anchor is often provided free, although you can buy one in bold type.

Worth Remembering

Don't waste money on a bold
telephone number in your listing.

Display Ads
(not actual size)

Quarter Page

Quarter Column

CHIROPRACTIC CLINIC
22014 7th Ave S ------------ 358-6600
(Please See Advertisement Page 231)

Anchor Listing
(must accompany
any Display ad)

Triple Quarter Column

33

WHICH ADS WORK BEST?

Listing Ads vs. Incolumn Space Ads. Incolumn space ads pull twice the number of customers as a bold listing. A listing gives the consumer your name, address and telephone number, but it does not begin to tell a story about your business. Customers generally want answers to questions before they buy. For this reason, space ads usually provide them with more of what they are seeking, increasing the chances they will call you over a competitor who draws the line at a listing.

If you only have a listing and a consumer wants to know if you are open evenings or if you carry a particular brand, why should he call you when your competitor answers that question in his ad? Since Incolumn space ads have twice the pulling power of listings, how much is doubling your potential business worth to you?

Consumers want information. It is easy to see why Incolumn Space Ads pull twice as much business as Listings.

Nationwide Loan Corp
Hwy 17 Little River............ 344-0509
Northwestern Mortgage Corp
2208 Azalea Court 326-6251
Pawn & Swap Shop
1304 N Main Cnwy............. 391-7676
Pee Dee Farm Credit Service
319 Beaty Cnwy 797-2030
People's Federal Savings & Loan Association
Accounting
212 Main Cnwy................. 764-0622

LOUIE'S PAWNSHOP
Established Since 1910
IMMEDIATE CASH LOAN OR BUY
Jewelry-Diamonds-Gold
Silver-Platinum-Objects D'Art
Estate Jewelry & Antiques
FREE APPRAISALS
LEGAL INTEREST RATES
Open Mon-Sat 9:30AM-6:00PM
1303 4th Av Conway.......626-7544

Incolumn Space Ads vs. Display Ads. The main advantage of Display advertising over advertising in the column is that it offers greater flexibility in layout and an opportunity to use impact headlines, distinctive borders and eye-catching illustrations.

Everyone has heard the saying, "One picture is worth a thousand words." Because a picture is more eye-commanding, it does a better job of grabbing the reader's attention. *"Where the eye stops, the sale begins"* is a fundamental of Yellow Pages advertising. When shoppers open the Yellow Pages, Display ads draw their attention first. This generally means more business for a Display advertiser than for an Incolumn advertiser.

It's easy to see why Display Ads get the most attention ...and the most business!

TAYLOR STEEL CORPORATION

DESIGN
FABRICATION
ERECTION

Service Call —————————293-9100

SILVIS STEEL
COMPANY

STEEL PRODUCTS IN
INVENTORY
REINFORCING RODS - WIRE MESH -

764-7779

2346 53rd Street   WAPELLO

Worth Remembering

*Center your telephone number in large, bold type
in the bottom one-third of your ad. This is
where shoppers will look for it.*

35

COMPARING ADS BY FUNCTION AND RATE

As you might expect, the larger the ad, the higher the monthly rate. A listing is rated lower than a 2-inch Incolumn space ad, which in turn is rated lower than a small Display ad. A small Display ad is rated lower than a larger Display ad, and so on. But the higher rate is not only because you get additional space. The chance to get more customers is *really* what you're paying more for.

As a rule, Incolumn space ads will pull in more business than listings, so they are rated higher. Display ads produce more customers than Incolumn ads do, so accordingly they have higher rates. But as always, there are exceptions to rules.

In checking, advertisers have sometimes been surprised to find that their Incolumn ads draw more customers for them than their Display ads. While this is unusual, there are situations in which an Incolumn ad will out-produce a Display ad. Here are some of them:

Active Heading: If the name of your business is Action Radiator or Carlson Towing, advertising in the column where ads are placed alphabetically will put you close to the start of a heading. At a very active heading, this will serve you better than a small Display ad which will have relatively poor position because there are so many ads there.

Flat Display Ad. A Display ad that packs no punch (called "flat" in the trade) can pull less effectively than a well-designed and carefully planned Incolumn ad.

Single Display Ad. A lone Display ad at a heading may end up placed on the page far from the heading it belongs to and can be overlooked as a result. You are much better off here with a more easily seen listing or Incolumn space ad that falls closer to the heading.

Gutter Ad. Since the response to an ad can be affected by where on a page it appears—unknown until the publisher has completely paged the directory prior to printing it—a Display ad that falls in the gutter (along the fold) can be overlooked in favor of a better placed Incolumn ad.

Bargain Hunters. Consumers sometimes respond to smaller Incolumn ads because they think they represent smaller companies who will do a job or offer a product at a lower price.

However, despite these occasional exceptions, Display ads generally get the best response. The following study illustrates just how much better.

Parker, the plumber, was given a Display ad, an Incolumn ad and a bold listing in a Yellow Pages directory. A different telephone number was placed in each ad, and the telephones were metered to count the calls. After one year, which brought in over 2,000 calls, the results were analyzed.

The Display ad generated approximately 7 of every 10 calls, the Incolumn ad produced 2 of 10, and the bold listing, only 1 of every 10. In short, the majority of consumers called from the Display ad.

While the Incolumn ad was responsible for only 20 percent of all calls, it still brought in twice as many as the listing. This is hardly a puzzle. As mentioned earlier, consumers go to the Yellow Pages seeking information. They are less likely to call you to ask if you carry a product or perform a service if another ad answers their question.

The results of this study are probably confirmed by your own experiences. Think about the last time you looked something up in the Yellow Pages and the ads that caught your attention first. In using the Yellow Pages in the future, notice which ads catch your eye. This is one of the best ways to learn what works in Yellow Pages advertising.

Worth Remembering

Remember the 7-2-1 ratio: From every 10 calls,
Display ads bring in 7, Space ads pull in 2,
and Listings, only 1.

Parker Plumbing Ad Response Test

One Year — Over 2,000 Calls

PARKER PLMBNG & HEATING CO.

SERVING ENTIRE AREA	PARKER PLUMBING

Complete Plumbing Repairs
New Installations — Water Heaters
Water Line Replacement
Call.................................299-5030

Incolumn Space Ad
Pulled 21% of all calls

PARKER PLMBNG & HEATING CO.
Call...299-3811

Bold Listing
Pulled 12% of all calls

38

REMODELING SPECIALISTS
KITCHEN • BATHROOM • HEATING

COMMERCIAL - INDUSTRIAL - RESIDENTIAL
• Heating • Cooling • Pumps • Electrical
• Water Heaters • Gas Piping

ESTIMATES • REASONABLE RATES • FHA TERMS

Parker **Plumbing & Heating Co.**

CALL ANY TIME DAY OR NIGHT...
299-5641

Display Ad
Pulled 67% of all calls

THE COMPARATIVE RATE FORMULA

Rates for the same sized ad vary dramatically from one directory or area to another. Whether the directory is an independent or telephone company publication, distribution figures and what the market will bear are factors that determine ad rates. In areas of the country where the Public Utilities Commission once regulated Yellow Pages advertising and controlled rate hikes, rates are lower (although they are rapidly catching up to those in areas that were never regulated.) These factors will be discussed at length later.

A bold listing may run a few dollars in one directory and as high as $25 in another. The largest Display ad offered in a directory, the one that gets you the best position, may run as low as $80 a month in a neighborhood book and as high as $2,500 in a directory that covers a large metropolitan area. This latter figure may shock some of you, but compare it to a price tag of $8,000 a month for a mobile billboard service in New York City, an advertising medium that produces far less exposure than an ad in the New York City Yellow Pages.

The National Yellow Pages Service Association (NYPSA) publishes a directory called *Rates & Data* that itemizes rates for every ad in every directory in the country. If you are interested, request a copy (NYPSA, 888 W. Big Beaver Road, Troy, Michigan 48084 Telephone (313) 362-3300). In the meantime, the following rule of thumb gives you an idea of how ad rates stack up against one another in the same directory.

The smallest Incolumn space ad is usually rated twice as high as a bold listing. Additional Incolumn space ads are rated by multiples of space. That is, a one-inch space ad runs twice the rate of a half-inch ad. A two-inch space ad is twice the rate of a one-inch ad, and so on. A Trademark ad is usually rated 5 times higher than a bold listing. A Custom Trademark, which is twice the size of a regular Trademark, is twice its price.

The Custom Trademark has a rate close to that of the smallest Display ad. Display ad rates go up according to multiples of the smallest ad. That is, an ad twice the size of the smallest is twice the rate. An ad four times the size of the smallest is four times the rate. Some directory companies lower the price of multiples as Display ads get larger, just as you save a bit when you buy the large economy size. But more common is to put a premium on top of what you would already expect to pay for a larger ad. That is, if the smallest Display ad is $100 per month, an ad 8 times its size might run $900 — 8 times $100 (the rate of the smallest Display ad) plus $100 for the premium. The premium pays for your gain in position.

COMPARATIVE RATE FORMULA

Comparing Ad Rates Within One Directory		
Incolumn Ads		
1/2" SPACE AD	= 2 x	Bold Listing
2" SPACE AD	= 2 x	1" Space Ad
4" SPACE AD	= 4 x	1" Space Ad
TRADEMARK	= 5 x	Bold Listing
CUSTOM TRADEMARK	= 2 x	Trademark
Display Ads		
QUARTER COLUMN (QC—Smallest)	= 1 x	Custom Trademark
DOUBLE QUARTER COLUMN (2 Times a QC in Area)	= 2 x	Quarter Column
DOUBLE HALF COLUMN (4 Times a QC in Area)	= 4 x	Quarter Column
HALF PAGE	= 8-10 x	Quarter Column (+ Premium)

DESIGNING AN EFFECTIVE INCOLUMN AD

Designing an effective Incolumn ad is a two-step process. You have to think about "THE LOOK" and "THE MESSAGE."

Step #1 is to create "The Look." The Look you want to create is one that will grab the eye and hold it. The reason for this is *"Where the eye stops, the sale begins."*

Step #2 is to successfully relay "The Message." *The goal is to target your specific markets and to provide all the complete buying information that will result in a sale.*

Whether you decide to do Display or Incolumn advertising, The Look and The Message must both be successful if a ready buyer is to become your customer.

The effect of having an ad without The Look usually tells in the results. Recall Clara Able of Ames Plumbing who had the misfortune to encounter a Yellow Pages salesperson in a hurry. He neglected to take a few minutes to give her ad some eye-appeal. As a result, Clara didn't get much business from the Yellow Pages during the year, despite the fact that the three plumbers who shared a page with her did very well indeed.

The following illustration shows why.

Worth Remembering

*Create your own ad. No one knows
your business (and your customers)
better than you do.*

YELLOW PAGES

Regional Telephone Directory

Ames Plumbing's Ad Lost Business

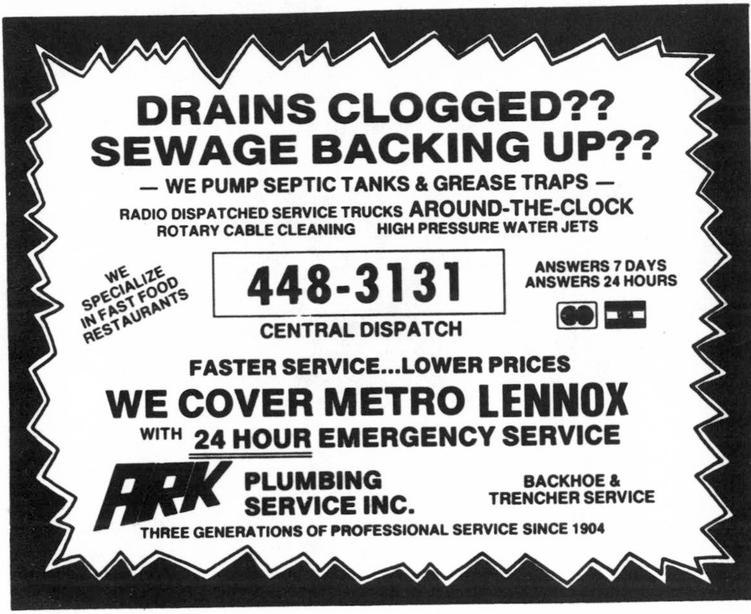

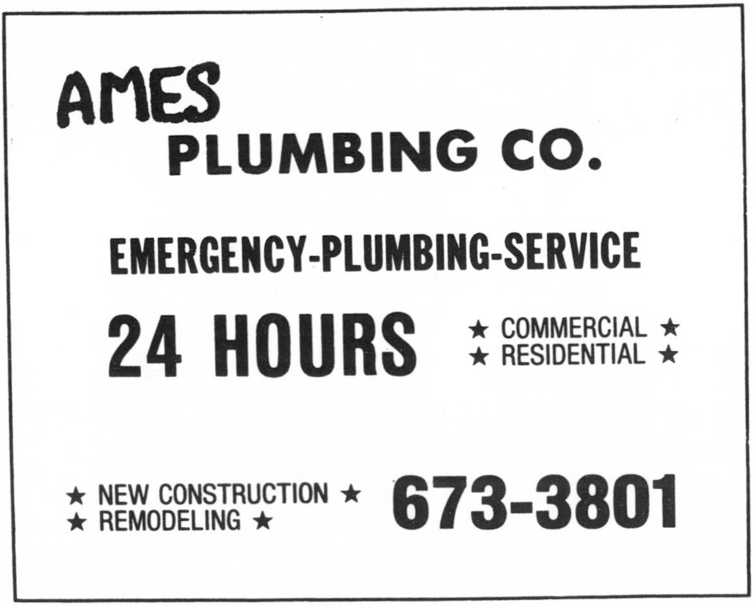

Because It Failed to Stop the Reader's Eye

Ads that lack The Message usually announce themselves by the complaints business owners make about the poor quality of the customers their ads are generating. They find respondents to their Yellow Pages ads inferior to customers brought in by referral or by word of mouth advertising. They accuse customers who call from the Yellow Pages of being bargain hunters or frequently wanting something their businesses do not sell. They are taken away from their work to answer the telephone and then receive nothing for their efforts.

The Yellow Pages has one job—making the telephone ring. Since more telephone calls result from the Yellow Pages than from any other form of advertising, they naturally bring in a larger share of nuisance calls. *What few people realize is that who responds to your advertising is something over which you have complete control—with the content of your ad.* An ad speaks. Your goal is to make it speak directly to the customers you want to attract.

Recall Jimmy Nelson, who repaired and replaced brakes. Because his ad didn't target his customers, it cost him time and money. He finally renewed his ad, accepting a suggestion to alter it by inserting a headline that read, "WHEN QUALITY IS YOUR FIRST CONCERN." In addition, he added to his copy, "My prices may be a bit higher, but what's a few dollars when your life is at stake?" He also put in some text describing the higher quality of his materials and the greater skill of his workers.

The following year Jimmy reported that while his telephone rang far fewer times than it had the year before, a much higher percentage of his calls turned into jobs. This, of course, meant a profitable investment for him.

The beauty of the Yellow Pages is that it offers an opportunity to design an ad that will elicit the types of customers that you want. A certain number of nuisance calls will result from any type of advertising, but they can be sharply reduced by targeting your ad.

JIMMY NELSON'S ADS

**NELSON'S BRAKES
FREE ESTIMATES**

**BRAKE SERVICE
WHEEL ALIGNMENT
WHEEL BALANCING
CLUTCH WORK**

637-1010
**9806 Candle Road
Petersburn**

OLD AD ... it pulled many calls, but few jobs.

**When QUALITY is your
first concern, call....**
NELSON'S BRAKES

• We use the finest materials
• Our workers are factory trained

**BRAKE SERVICE
WHEEL ALIGNMENT
WHEEL BALANCING
CLUTCH WORK**

"My rates may be a bit higher, but what's a few dollars when your life is at stake?"
637-1010
**9806 Candle Road
Petersburn**

NEW AD ... it pulled fewer calls, but most of them became jobs.

THE LOOK

Even though Display ads pull from 55 percent to 85 percent of customer responses (depending upon which survey you refer to), Incolumn ads are appropriate in certain situations. Perhaps the low activity at a heading does not warrant Display advertising. Or you may do Display advertising at your major heading and advertise in the column at secondary headings. In either case, the Incolumn ad must have The Look if it is to do its job.

Incolumn ads consist primarily of text, except for a logo or small illustration. Therefore, The Look must be achieved with the size, style and layout of the type. Ad size determines the maximum number of lines or words of text permitted.

Follow these rules:

RULE #1 Use as few words and lines of text as possible. This will permit you to double the type size and make it bolder. The result is a more eye-catching, readable message.

RULE #2 Vary type sizes and styles and lengths of lines.

RULE #3 Use bullets or asterisks to set off different ideas.

When you finally decide on a particular Incolumn ad, your salesperson will bring out a form called a Copysheet. This will be used for the layout of your ad. It is critical that you provide a sample of each size and style of type you want to use. While you and your salesperson may be clear on what it is you want, neither one of you will be present when the typesetter does her work. Unfortunately, camera ready artwork is not accepted for Incolumn, ads which are now generally set by computer.

This...

PHOENIX SALES COMPANY
NAME BRAND FURNITURE
WHOLESALE TO ANYONE
CONVENIENT LAYAWAY
PLAN
MAJOR CREDIT CARDS
ACCEPTED
FINE GIFT WARE
305 Flagg 448-8141

Not This

MEDICAL CENTER
INTERNAL MEDICINE
In House LAB, X-RAY, EKG, SPIROMETRY
SIGMOIDOSCOPE, AUDIOMETRY,
CARDIAC MONITORING-For Industry we offer:
EXECUTIVE PHYSICALS - TREATMENT OF
MINOR EMERGENCIES - WORKMAN'S COMP
INJURY TREATMENT - OFFICE
HOURS BY APPOINTMENT
Hwy 501 448-8568

This...

TAYLOR WHOLESALE
DIAMONDS
COLORED GEMSTONES
DIRECT FROM THE CUTTER
G.I.A. APPRAISALS - MOUNTINGS
BY APPOINTMENT TO THE PUBLIC
FREE INFORMATION
.... 448-9483

Not This

BAGWELL COURIERS
Small Pkg Spec • Radio Dispatched
Insured • Carry Up To 500 Lbs.
Immediate Pickup & Delivery Anytime
2 Seagull Blvd 249-2111

This...

LIBERTY HOUSE

Providing

PARTY PERSONNEL
Bonded & Insured
• BARTENDERS
• SERVERS
• HOSTESSES
• MODELS

LIBERTY
HOUSE

• ICE SCULPTURES
• LIMOUSINES
• DISC JOCKEYS
• PHOTOGRAPHERS
ACTS: MIMES-CLOWNS-MAGIC

Liberty House
2205 W 6th St LosAngeles ------**380-6090**

Not This

P SHARP ASSOCIATES

25 Years Experience-General Contractors-Finance
Easily Taken Care Of-Roofs
Room Additions-Siding-Gutters-Burglar Bars-Heating
& Air Conditioning Contractors-Storm
Window & Window Replacement-Driveways,
Patios And Patchwork-Painting Contractors
"PLEASE CALL
FOR MORE INFORMATION"

P Sharp Associates Inc
1776 Briarcliff Rd NE ------ **244-3006**

If you are not familiar with type sizes or the names of print styles, printers and typesetters often give away brochures that illustrate them. Or find similar sizes and styles in the Yellow Pages, cut them out, and watch as they are pasted directly on to the copysheet.

Carefully read every word that is written on the copysheet, double checking it for accuracy. Advance copies or proofs (facsimiles of ads sent to you for viewing before the printing of the directory) are available only to Display ad vertisers, not to Incolumn advertisers. If a word is misspelled or incorrect on your copysheet, it may very well appear that way in the directory. Now is the last chance you will have to make any changes or corrections.

Important: *Before your salesperson leaves, get a copy of the copysheet for your records.* If you do not have a copier, have her go to a printer to make a copy for you. Salespeople are notorious for putting finishing touches to your ad before submitting it to the publisher. Should this happen to you, only your photocopy will serve as proof that you did not get what you signed for.

THE MESSAGE

Since readers tend to read from top to bottom, that is how the lines of text in an Incolumn ad should be prioritized. The most important information should appear closest to the top. In addition, larger and bolder print will outshine smaller, light type print; and capital letters will stand out more than upper/lower case.

It is also vital that you target your customers. While you have less space here than in a Display ad, you should still use it to make sure that your text speaks to those people you want to talk to. If low prices is your strong suit, feature it prominently at the top of your ad. It will attract price shoppers. If a big selection is your drawing card, say so.

DESIGNING AN EFFECTIVE DISPLAY AD

Pick up a Yellow Pages directory and thumb through it. Be conscious of the Display ads that catch your eye. What drew you to a particular ad? Was it a striking border, or the large, commanding bold print? Did a pleasing design, a photograph or some snappy illustrations catch your attention? All these are critical elements in creating The Look. And they work.

HOW DISPLAY ADS ARE BORN

Sometimes an advertiser hires an agency or some other professional to create an ad for him, but most ads you see in the Yellow Pages are composed by Yellow Pages personnel who have been trained in this area.

If you already have an ad, the salesperson may make a suggestion or two to improve upon it. If you don't have one, a salesperson has several courses to follow to develop one for you.

Most Yellow Pages companies employ artists who prepare ads for potential buyers. Salespeople, in turn, employ these ads as sales tools, using them in persuading you to buy. If the salesperson has some artistic ability, she may draw an ad on her own. But by far the majority of ads that you see in the Yellow Pages came about by cutting and pasting.

A salesperson chooses a Yellow Pages directory from a distant area. She then selects an ad from your heading that has a unique border and some attractive or original illustration. She cuts out the identifying name, address and telephone number and perhaps adds some text to personalize the ad to your business. She pastes all this on to a copysheet, and Presto! You have an ad.

This method of creating Display ads can cause problems. An insurance agent found the ad he had used successfully for many years duplicated by an agent new to the area. To worsen matters, the new agent had purchased an ad larger than the original. Since larger ads are positioned ahead of smaller ones, shoppers saw the new agent's ad first. An investigation revealed that an inexperienced salesperson was to blame for using a local directory to cut artwork for another local business. A lawsuit is still pending against the new agent, the salesperson and the Yellow Pages.

You now know how Yellow Pages salespeople create Display Ads. It is not difficult—you can do it, too. To avoid having someone "borrow" any elements from your ad once you have gone to the trouble of creating it, here is a tip.

Anything in your ad that you wish to reserve forever as your own should be followed by the mark of registry ® or copyright ©. Even though it may not be registered or copyrighted, it will be safe. For obvious reasons, Yellow Pages salespeople usually steer clear of anything in an ad that is so marked.

CREATING YOUR OWN AD

It is imperative that you take responsibility and become involved in the ad creating process. First, it takes a long time to learn all the ins and outs of the Yellow Pages, and today is some Yellow Pages salesperson's first day of the rest of his career. Inexperience may cause him, despite good intentions, to make up an ad for you that doesn't work. Second, some salespeople never learn how to create an ad that is a money maker, no matter how long they are on the job. Third, in the interest of saving time, some salespeople will slap together any old thing just to get the job done. Finally, there are salespeople who do not care if your ad works or not. Since they only plan to make a few dollars and then move on to greener pastures, the fact that you will not get any business and refuse to renew your advertising next year is of little consequence to them.

For these reasons, it is crucial that you become adept at recognizing the elements that make an ad an eye-grabber and not depend upon your salesperson to do the job for you. Look at the artwork she has, listen to her suggestions, but ultimately take responsibility for your own ad.

AD DESIGN AND LAYOUT

In Display ads, The Look catches the buyer's attention through borders, illustrations, large, bold print, screens/reverses, and photographs. It holds that attention and favorably inclines it toward your business through the use of pleasing ad format.

The Message continues the sale already set in motion. You target clearly those groups of buyers who will be disposed to do business with you. You also need copy factors that supply complete buying information to the consumer.

At this point, an invitation in your ad to that ready buyer—drop in, call for an appointment, visit our showroom—is all that is needed to make a customer of him.

Relying on your Yellow Pages salesperson to know and to be willing to go through this process for you is a big mistake. Your input is crucial. She may know businesses in general, but only you know *your* business.

Your ad must be an attention getter. It must be personalized, reflecting the markets you want to target and the groups you are best suited to serve. It must feature the special services that distinguish you from your competitors. Otherwise, it will not do the job.

Borders. An outstanding border is one of the most effective ways to attract the eye. Some directory companies have a collection of standard borders from which they encourage you to choose. This saves on their costs. While many of these borders are effective, if you do not find one that you like, pick one directly from the Yellow Pages. Following are borders that are proven items.

Worth Remembering

People tend to read from left to right, top to bottom. Keep this in mind when you arrange the elements in your ad.

Theme borders: Flowers for florists, drain pipes for plumbers and frames for picture dealers are not only eye-catching but quickly announce to the reader that he has found what he is looking for.

Bakery

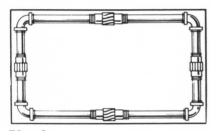

Plumber

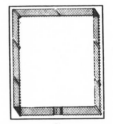

Fence Contractor

Florist

Picture Framer

Stand-out borders: Checkerboards, flames and stars, while old hat, draw the eye.

Brand name borders: Tell the reader what brands you service by making a border that announces them.

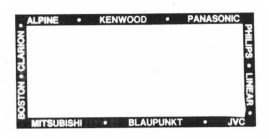

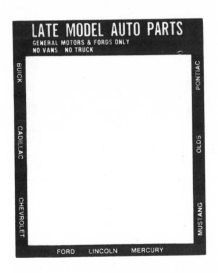

Hairline borders: This border is appropriate if your ad is small and you need all available space for text and illustrations, or if the logos and pictures in your ad would lose impact against a flashy border.

To further emphasize their impact, compare the ads below —
identical except for their borders.

The Eye-Catching Power
of a Border

Identical Ad — Different Border

Illustrations. Illustrations add to your text, enhance the appearance of your ad, and stop the reader's eye. Relate illustrations to what you are trying to sell. If a shopper is thinking "I need more lighting for this room," let her open the Yellow Pages to the heading and be drawn by the illustrations of lamps in your ad.

You may have camera ready artwork that will maximize the chances of your getting exactly what you want. If not, tell your salesperson what illustrations you want, and he can have the publisher draw them for you. But be specific. To simply say you want a car is to court trouble. Artists do their work well, but they are not mind readers. Ask for a Buick of 1960 vintage and mention the model. Better yet, provide a picture from a brochure or magazine that the artist can improve upon.

Line drawings, illustrations composed of solid black and white lines with no shading or screening involved, are very effective. Clip art is available to you by the book or sheet and consists of line drawings on almost every conceivable subject.

Line Drawings

Art may also be taken from old magazines or books, and anything printed before 1956 is probably safe from copyright protection. But by far the best source of illustrations is—you guessed it, the Yellow Pages.

When you travel, always cut out unusual ads from Yellow Pages directories you find in your hotel room. Have out-of-town friends send you unique ads from their local directories. This will guarantee not only that you get something different, but that you don't duplicate ads already under your heading.

Always check the headings in the directories you plan to advertise in to make sure illustrations you plan to use are not already being used by a competitor. Additionally, be sure to bypass any illustration or slogan that has the copyright or registered mark following it.

Screens and Reverse. Screening is a method of shading or tinting. Reverse is a 100 percent screen and appears black. Both are effective in drawing the reader's attention. To prove this to yourself, find ads that employ these processes in the Yellow Pages and compare them to other ads that lack these features.

Line Drawing with Screen

Reverse in Headline

Directory companies have rules about the percentages of screening they will allow. In addition, many directory companies do not permit the use of reverse, other than in a very small space, because during the printing process the concentrated ink tends to bleed through and discolor ads on nearby pages. When you decide on the degree of screening that you want to use, don't settle for the salesperson's writing "dark screen" or "light screen" on the copysheet. Cut out a sample of what you want from the Yellow Pages and paste it on to the copysheet. You may know what you mean by "dark," but the publisher may have a different idea.

Photographs (half-tones). Photographs definitely have eye-interest, but in general, they do not produce well in the Yellow Pages. The worst part is that they are unpredictable. What looks like a good, clear photograph to you may look blurred, too dark or faded out when it appears it in your ad. If you decide to use a photograph, keep in mind that high contrast works best. Make sure it is black and white with the utmost clarity to increase the chances that it will reproduce well. Color prints reproduced in black and white tend to acquire a muddy appearance. Any photograph you submit can be returned to you after use, provided you tell your salesperson.

For examples of the range of clarity found in reproduced photographs, turn to the "Insurance" or "Photographers" headings. They tend to carry more photographs than any others and underline the problems of reproducing photographs in the Yellow Pages.

Large, Bold Print. The ads that caught your attention probably employed large, bold print, which is easily readable. Use white print on a screen for extra impact. Always request that print on a screen be outlined. This will prevent it from having a blurry appearance.

Color Ink. As you look through the ads at a heading, you may notice another Yellow Pages innovation—type or illustration in red ink. Directory companies that offer red ink claim it creates greater interest in your ad and has higher impact on the consumer than the more common black ink. This, they say, leads to more business.

The facts are that approximately one-half of advertisers who try red ink find it makes no difference in the amount of business their ads bring them and discontinue it the following year. Red ink increases the cost of an ad by approximately 50 percent, and businesses claim that the results simply do not warrant it. (An irony of this situation is that printers say red ink costs less than its black counterpart!)

Used judiciously, however, red ink can make a difference in certain situations. The more ads on a page, the greater clout the only ad with red ink will have in drawing a shopper's eye. If you plan an Incolumn ad or a small Display ad that would tend to get lost at a highly active heading, red ink will serve you well. Large Display ads that have good positioning and compete with only a few other large ads get poor mileage from red ink considering its high cost. Even in a small ad, red ink can backfire if too many advertisers use it. The result is that black ink now has more impact.

Directory companies are currently experimenting with a new printing process that will allow them to use a variety of colors in the Yellow Pages. This will have the effect of driving rates up and forcing advertisers to participate in multi-color advertising in order to stay competitive. With some luck, it may go the way of other innovative flops—coupons and full-page color inserts.

Layout. The importance of the layout of your ad is that once the ad's elements have gained the reader's attention, an eye-pleasing layout will hold that attention. It is a challenge to lay out an effective ad because of the conflict that arises between including all necessary information and not making the ad so busy that it is less likely to be read. An additional problem enters the picture because surveys indicate that unless you specifically mention a product or service in your ad, shoppers assume you do not provide it. A compromise must be struck between these two factors.

Worth Remembering

Always outline type that appears on a screen or reverse background. It will keep words from having a blurry look.

The rules to follow for visually aesthetic Display ad design are:

RULE #1 Start with a center of interest to emphasize one of your more important elements, and work around it.

RULE #2 Limit the number of elements such as headlines, lists, and slogans, and simplify them as much as possible.

RULE #3 Group common elements, such as lists of brand names, to create an organized and easily read ad.

RULE #4 Employ the use of open space—it encourages reading.

RULE #5 As in Incolumn ads, employ varied type sizes and styles for interest.

If you find a particularly good layout in someone else's ad, be guided by it. Should you attempt your own layout without the help of a salesperson, show your efforts to your staff and to friends and family to get their impressions. After all, they are consumers, too.

If you follow these rules, your Display ad will have THE LOOK necessary to capture the attention of potential customers. Once you have their attention, you only have a matter of seconds to make sure you keep it. THE MESSAGE must now speak to them.

This...

RENT TO OWN • SALES • SERVICE

COMPLETE SERVICE ON ALL MAKES

• ZENITH
• RCA
• MAGNAVOX
• QUASAR
• PHILCO
• SONY

A&B TELEVISION

• SHARP
• TELEDYNE
• SYLVANIA
• SANYO
• HITACHI
• TATUNG

SINCE 1960

"We Sell the Best and service the rest"

448-9938

MON-FRI 9-6
SAT 10-5

VILLAGE SQUARE SHOPPING CENTER

Not This

TARGETING YOUR MARKETS

While almost everyone receives a copy of the Yellow Pages, only a percentage is your target market—those persons whom you want to attract or who would have a reason to deal specifically with you. It is obvious that you cannot be everything to all people.

If you are a building contractor, consider what kinds of customers you want to draw. What type of building do you enjoy most? Do you prefer remodeling jobs, or do you like the challenge of building an entire structure from scratch? What part of the marketplace do you want to capture? Residences? Industrial complexes? Commercial establishments?

Only after you have answered these questions (as they translate to your particular business) and determined the customers you want to target most can you select the approach and key words and phrases that will speak directly to these groups of people.

Earlier you read about a business that repaired and replaced brakes. The owner was able to replace nuisance calls with productive ones by changing the focus of his ad from "FREE ESTIMATES" to a headline that read "WHEN QUALITY IS YOUR FIRST CONCERN." The new focus more accurately reflected what he was offering and attracted customers more likely to do business with him—those who put quality before cost.

Suppose you are a refrigerator dealer. There are a number of reasons why people might buy a refrigerator: to replace a broken one, for their first home, to upgrade to a newer model, for a second residence, or to suit a remodeled kitchen.

But why would these people choose *you* to deal with? Perhaps you offer discount prices or a large selection of brand names. The fact that you guarantee your merchandise, have a convenient location, or carry a particular model may persuade others.

Who are the customers that you most want to attract? Because you feature discount prices, one target group is people concerned with cost. Your brand names would draw in people seeking a particular brand, providing a second target group. A convenient location would draw shoppers who wanted a nearby outlet to deal with. Hence, a third target group. Merchandise guarantees might attract people concerned with reliable service. Target group Number 4. And so on.

You must now prioritize your target groups according to their degree of match with what you are offering and allocate space in your Display ad accordingly. If low price is your main draw, "LOW PRICES" must receive prominent position and major space in your ad. Shoppers looking for discount prices will hear your shout as they look at your ad.

Use the pie below to pinpoint the customers you want to target. Then look at the following pies and notice how the ads created from them speak to the customers each business hopes to attract. Make sure your ad does this, too.

**Use This Pie to
Plan your ad. What
Customers Do You Want
to Target?**

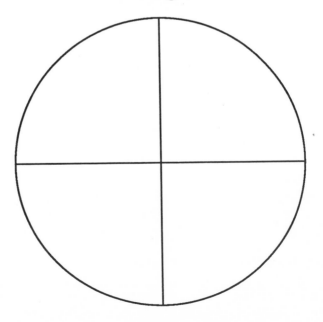

Optometrist #1
Customers he wants to target

People in a hurry

Others

Price Shoppers

People Concerned with Location

Space in ad targets desired customers.
Higher priorities get more space.

Optometrist #2
Customers she wants to target

**Space in ad targets desired customers.
Higher priorities get more space.**

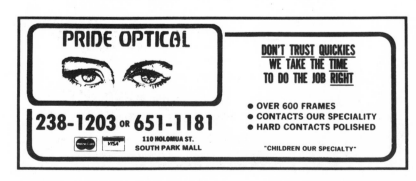

Headlines. "Headline" is the term given to the banner-like area you find at the top of many of the Display ads in the Yellow Pages. Appearing at the top of the ad where people begin to read gives it tremendous potential clout. Yet the headline is the most misused ad space in the Yellow Pages.

Many businesses use the headline to shout their names to the public, even though in most cases few have ever heard of Johnson Brothers' Painting or Allen Copiers or Jill Squill, Attorney. The real function of the headline is to promote what you are selling, to highlight the service or specialty offered.

When consumers use the Yellow Pages, they generally have a specific need. As they browse, their attention is more likely to be drawn to words that describe their problem rather than to a name. A customer seeking discount prices is more likely to respond to a headline that reads "SOME OF THE LOWEST PRICES IN TOWN" rather than to one that heralds "JOHN'S REFRIGERATORS." The former headline virtually cries out to the shopper's need, and the ad has successfully targeted a customer.

Headlines that Work
They Target Their Most
Important Market and Sell to It!

For a Dentist...

For a Hardware Store...
HARD TO FIND HARDWARE

For a Mover...

ASK ABOUT OUR
MONEY-BACK
GUARANTEE
"YEARS OF PROFESSIONAL SERVICE"

For a Nursery School...

"Hey, Mom & Dad..
Our Future is
in your Hands."

For a Chiropractor...

ARE YOU IN PAIN?

Addressing your ad to the markets you want to target puts you halfway towards your goal of relaying THE MESSAGE. The full job is achieved by including in your ad the seven important copy factors that provide most of the information shoppers look for when they go to the Yellow Pages. These copy factors are known in the industry as the RASCALS.

THE RASCALS. RASCALS is an acronym representing the seven key copy factors that increase the chances a buyer will respond to your ad.

R: Reliability. This includes such information as the number of years in business (Since 1954), the size of the firm (3 locations to serve you), references (over 10,000 satisfied customers), and licenses (State Contractor's Lic. #3035).

A: Authorized sales and service: Brand names you handle influence buyers already exposed to national advertising in other media (We Service Brands A, B, C and D).

S: Safety and protection. These are points that reassure potential buyers that their property is protected from harm: Fully insured and bonded, Factory trained workers, All Workmanship guaranteed.

C: Completeness of line or service: These factors have to do with the range and variety of stock, business hours, days open, credit, delivery, etc. (We carry all major brands, Open 7 days a week, All credit cards accepted).

A: Artwork: Illustrations, emblems, slogans or logos are all helpful in depicting products or services offered.

L: Location: Buyers are influenced by location, tending to look for convenient or nearby sources for their needs. Specifics such as maps, Across from City Hall, On the Corner of Fifth and Main, etc., help the buyer to locate you.

S: Special Services. This is your opportunity to promote a competitive difference, to show the buyer what distinguishes *you* from others in your line. Award-winning restaurants, a dry cleaner who preserves wedding gowns, a hardware store that gives free advice to do-it-yourselfers all have good opportunities here.

71

Use the Advertising Copy Guide checklist to pinpoint the RASCALS that apply to your business and ensure that your ad has the pulling power it needs.

ADVERTISING COPY GUIDE

RELIABILITY
Years in business...........Years of experience.............
Number of locations......References......License #'s......

AUTHORIZED BRAND NAMES (Sales/Service)
....
....

SAFETY & PROTECTION — Bonded — Insured
Guarantees...................Worker Training.......................

COMPLETENESS OF SERVICE
Retail...Whsle...Residential...Commercial...Industrial....
Variety/Selection...
Market Area...
Delivery Service..
Days Open...
Hours Open..
Emergency Service Available.....................................
Credit/Credit Cards...
Estimates..............Any charge?..............................
Mail/Telephone Orders...
Parking Facilities..

ARTWORK
Logos/Emblems............Illustrations........................
Association Cuts..........Slogans.............................

LOCATIONS
Nearby landmarks..
Intersection/Highway No.......................................
Map Necessary...

SPECIAL SERVICES (What I have or offer that other businesses like mine don't)
Awards..
Customer Incentives...
Unique Items..
Attractive prices...
Other...
Which products or services are most important or offer the greatest profit potential?..............................
What market areas are my best?.................................

Examine the ads below. Which has the information that will increase the chances that shoppers will become customers? What RASCALS is the other lacking?

YES	NO	
☐	☐	**Reliability** Years in business, size of firm, references, number of locations, licenses
☐	☐	**Authorized Sales and Service** Brands names sold and serviced
☐	☐	**Safety and Protection** Insured, Bonded, Guarantees
☐	☐	**Completeness of Service** Stock, hours/days open, credit, delivery
☐	☐	**Artwork** Illustrations, emblems, slogans, logos
☐	☐	**Location** Maps or other locations
☐	☐	**Special Features** Unique services

We use the most updated equipment

★ OUR TRUCK-MOUNTED STEAM METHOD IS BETTER THAN SHAMPOO, PORTABLE STEAM OR DRY CLEANING.

★ OUR METHOD REMOVES MORE DIRT THAN OTHER METHODS AND LEAVES NO RESIDUE ON YOUR CARPET OR FURNITURE. NO SOAKING OR SHRINKAGE.

RESIDENTIAL • COMMERCIAL

Vince's
CARPET CLEANING
833-7872

YES	NO	
❏	❏	**Reliability** Years in business, size of firm, references, number of locations, licenses
❏	❏	**Authorized Sales and Service** Brands names sold and serviced
❏	❏	**Safety and Protection** Insured, Bonded, Guarantees
❏	❏	**Completeness of Service** Stock, hours/days open, credit, delivery
❏	❏	**Artwork** Illustrations, emblems, slogans, logos
❏	❏	**Location** Maps or other locations
❏	❏	**Special Features** Unique services

WHAT YOU CANNOT PUT IN YOUR AD

There may be times when you want to include some text in your ad but cannot. Yellow Pages companies have rules about what constitutes acceptable ad copy, which vary from one company to another. Some rules are accepted by advertisers as reasonable and seldom create problems, such as those prohibiting advertisers from expressing prejudicial attitudes in ad copy. Other rules, however, frequently come into conflict with what advertisers want to do. The more common ones include:

Residential Lines: In order to be listed as a business or to advertise in telephone company directories, you are required to have a business telephone line. Independent directory companies are more flexible, allowing you to use a home telephone line for directory advertising. Because of the expense involved in installing and maintaining a business telephone, people who operate businesses from their homes often restrict their advertising to independent directories.

Rotary Telephone Numbers: If you have three telephone numbers in sequence, such as 821-6401, 821-6402, and 821-6403, chances are the first is a primary number and the other two are rotary lines. The second two lines will ring in turn if the previous line is in use.

Directory companies do not normally permit you to use a rotary number in Yellow Pages ads unless your primary number is also listed, although it can appear in the smallest sized type. The reason for this is that poor initial results from your advertising may motivate you to disconnect a rotary line to avoid paying your bill. Disconnecting a rotary line usually causes you only minor inconvenience as it is your primary number that your customers know.

Directory companies have a difficult time making a case in court that an advertiser who has disconnected the telephone number in his ad is benefiting, and their chances of collecting are low.

Aside from the few advertisers who deliberately use a rotary number in their ads with the idea in mind of disconnecting it later and leaving the bill unpaid, others want to use a rotary number to test the results of their advertising. But a rotary number is not an effective means of doing this, as you will learn.

Fraudulent or Misleading Information: Information which is fraudulent or misleading, which reflects discredit on competitors, which is offensive to good taste or which offers excessive gain or similar questionable inducements is not permitted in ad copy.

Information Opposed to Federal and State Laws: Certain rules reflect the law and are observed in Yellow Pages advertising. An example is the necessity for contractors to include their license numbers in any advertising they do. Salespeople have little means at their disposal of policing this and usually fail to verify that someone really is a contractor. As a result, non-licensed individuals do slip in.

One very successful salesperson makes a habit of fabricating fictitious license numbers for her non-contractor advertisers. This enables them to take a shortcut to legitimacy and advertise under the lucrative contractor headings. It also helps to increase her sales. Understandably, this is a big irritant to legitimate contractors, and they are quick to blow the whistle on these non-contractor interlopers.

Superlatives: Any guarantees or use of superlatives in your ad ("Money-back Guarantees," "The lowest prices in town" or "The oldest dealership in the city") are likely to lead to a request that you sign a disclaimer. The primary purpose of this rule is to hold the directory company harmless from lawsuits, but it also attempts to protect you should your claim be proven wrong during the life of the directory. The largest dealership today will not be the largest tomorrow if someone opens a larger one.

Photograph Releases: Written permission is usually needed from people appearing in photographs that are to be reproduced in the Yellow Pages.

Addresses in Ads: Businesses operating from a residence usually do not want their addresses to appear in their ads or listings. For the protection of consumers, some directory companies require that businesses involved in the removal of property from a consumer's home—such as a mover, a carpet cleaner, or an upholsterer—must publish their addresses in their ads or listings. Other directory companies leave this to the discretion of the advertiser, unless required by law.

Ad Sharing: Sometimes two or more businesses want to pool their resources and share a large ad to gain position. This is generally not permitted unless the businesses are commonly owned. It must then be clearly indicated in the ad that they are under the same ownership.

Prices: Ad copy usually may not contain prices, price ranges, percent reductions or percent discounts, interest or repayment tables. Even if you could include this information in your ad, it would probably not be a good idea. If you should change any of these figures during the life of the directory, you could incur a lawsuit from a disgruntled customer.

Statements About Credit: The Truth in Lending Act, made law in 1969, makes certain statements about credit unacceptable. For example, "Charge accounts available" is permitted, but "No money down" is not; "Terms arranged" is allowed, but "Finance for under $50" is not. Your salesperson can advise you on how to phrase text so that it will be accepted.

Unauthorized Trademarks / Tradenames: Reference to trademarks or tradenames of another may be made if you can show that you are authorized. Where no authority exists, businesses often get around this by stating, "Specialists in Honda Repair" or "Expert Service on General Electric products."

Other rules for unacceptable copy exist but come up rarely. Your salesperson or the publisher will inform you if any part of your ad content has transgressed policy.

POSITION: HOW IMPORTANT IS IT?

The story goes in the real estate business that people buying property need only consider three things: Location, location and location. In the Yellow Pages industry, there is parallel advice for Display advertisers: Position, position and position.

Position is of critical importance in Yellow Pages advertising. Since consumers who use the Yellow Pages typically start reading at the beginning of a heading and work their way back, where your ad is placed in relationship to where the heading starts is very important.

When consumers pick up the Yellow Pages without a particular business in mind, they usually turn to the heading and begin to read. The closer your ad is to the start of the heading, the sooner it is read. The farther back your ad is, the greater the chance that the consumer will find what he needs without ever seeing your ad.

Consumers might read the smaller ads, thinking they represent smaller businesses with lower prices. Sometimes they shop all ads at a heading, looking for a nearby location or a specialty item. But the evidence suggests that the larger ads, because of their prime positioning, reap most of the business that comes from a heading.

The more ads at a heading, the more critical positioning becomes. Being visible quickly is very important since half the people using the Yellow Pages will be persuaded by another business's advertising if they have any difficulty finding you.

The dilemma facing a new Display advertiser at an active heading is at once apparent. It is not surprising that they often buy established businesses at outrageous prices. Since ad position generally is tied to a telephone number, the new business inherits the former business's ad position.

Yellow Pages companies are aware that the battle for position gives them yet another opportunity to increase their revenues. They frequently escalate the position war by offering even a larger ad. You are forced to buy this bigger ad or lose position.

Some advertisers believe that people shop from the end of a heading and move forward, and they insist on being the last ad at a heading. But the facts do not bolster this theory.

Research on how ad size affects the number of customers produced suggests that the largest ads get the best results. Further, even though ad rate increases arithmetically (twice the space costs twice as much), effectiveness increases geometrically. In other words, an ad twice the size will produce 5, not 2, times the response. An ad 4 times the size will produce 15, not 4, times the result.

IMPACT OF AD SIZE ON CUSTOMER RESPONSE

4 Times as Big as Ⓐ
Rated approximately four times as much
15 TIMES AS EFFECTIVE

Twice as Big as Ⓐ
Rated approximately twice as much
5 TIMES AS EFFECTIVE

Smallest Display Ad

While Display advertisers tend to confirm that at a very active heading the larger ads produce better, business people make money from ads of all sizes. This is true because factors other than position determine how successful an ad is, as you will find out.

HOW ADS ARE POSITIONED

The major difference between Display ads and Incolumn ads is that Incolumn ads are positioned alphabetically while Display ads are grouped by size and seniority.

The largest Display ads are positioned first. If you are a Display advertiser, particularly at an active heading, you must be very concerned with the position of your ad.

In addition to the larger ads being placed closer to the start of a heading, Display ads are ordered on the basis of seniority within each size grouping. The quarter column ad purchased first is positioned first, and ads of this size bought later are positioned behind it according to the date of purchase. (In the rare case that the same sized ads at a heading are purchased on the same day, the decision is made alphabetically according to the names of the businesses.)

Preferential positioning is sometimes given to local businesses during the early stages of a sales campaign, with advertisers outside the area being sorted in later. Many non-local advertisers overcome this obstacle to good positioning by installing a local telephone number, which qualifies them as a local business.

Buying the largest Display ad available is the only way to guarantee your position. Any size other than the largest means that someone buying an ad larger than yours at any time in the future is positioned ahead of you. If an ad larger than any previously offered is introduced later, you must buy it or lose your favored position.

With the largest ad, your position can only improve. As other advertisers close their doors, move out of the area, elect not to renew their advertising or reduce their ad size, you move ahead.

Certain placement on a page is preferable because people tend to read from top to bottom and from left to right. In order, the best page placement is top left, top right, bottom left, and bottom right. Unfortunately, there is nothing you can do to have your ad placed at any particular spot on a page. Where it appears is strictly a matter of chance.

Smaller ads sometimes fall in the the gutter, the fold where the book is bound. Since some people hold the directory in the crook of their arm, causing the gutters to touch, ads placed here can be overlooked. Larger ads are seldom placed in the gutter. This is yet another way that directory companies encourage you to buy a larger ad.

IMPROVING YOUR POSITION

One way to improve the position of your Display ad is, of course, to buy a bigger one. If there are already many large Display ads at your heading, even buying the largest ad will not automatically give you an attractive position. You may just have to buy your place in line and wait for the years to take their toll on better-positioned businesses.

There are, however, some little known ways to gain a position advantage without putting more money out of pocket, whether you do Display advertising or stick to Incolumn ads.

Incolumn Ads. Some advertisers have caught on to a method of appearing close to the start of a heading in the column and gaining a competitive edge, regardless of the name of their business.

If you look up the active heading "Plumbing Contractors," you will notice a number of listings for companies with names like AAA Plumbing, A-1 Plumbing, or AAAA-E-Z Plumbers. Not all these companies had the foresight when starting in business to keep Yellow Pages positioning in mind.

Instead, they fabricate a business name that begins with the letter "A," which gives them an alphabetical advantage. For consumers who have no firm in mind when they open the Yellow Pages, the name of a business is of little importance. Businesses that use this strategy should also list their true business name so that regular and referral customers can find them.

Some directory companies are on to this ruse and now require you to produce a legal DBA for any business name under which you list in the Yellow Pages. Depending on how active your heading is, it may be worthwhile to acquire a DBA to get a more forward position in the column. Again, don't forget to list under your legitimate business name as well for the benefit of regular customers and referrals.

It goes without saying that anyone starting a new business, particularly one in which Yellow Pages will play a critical role, should name his business with this in mind. Zebra Plumbing is bound to lose customers to Antelope Plumbing when shoppers look in the column for a business to deal with.

Display Ads. In Display advertising, "heading jumping" is the name given to a scheme that enables a business to enormously improve the position of a Display ad without spending an extra dime.

Many extremely competitive headings have a less active one just preceding it. An example of this is "Refrigerating Equipment-Commercial-Sales and Service" that directly precedes "Refrigerators & Freezers-Dealers and Service," a more competitive heading.

If you are in the business of repairing refrigerators for both residential and commercial establishments but the bulk of your business is residential, your ad would normally be placed at "Refrigerators and Freezers-Dealers and Service." This lucrative heading is crammed with large Display ads, putting the newcomer to it at a big disadvantage.

The heading that comes just before it, "Refrigerating Equipment-Commercial-Sales and Service," is far less active. An ad placed at this heading, even though it might not truly reflect your business, would "jump ahead" of all the ads at the more active heading.

Heading jumping works because Yellow Pages users are often too hurried or unaware to differentiate between two similar headings. A heading jumper is gambling that the shopper will not read the full heading , but see the word "Refrigerator" and assume he has reached the right place. If illustrations and text in your ad are geared to both commercial and residential markets, chances are you can still enjoy a fair amount of residential business from your ad, even though it appears at a heading that caters to commercial establishments.

Rampant heading jumping also occurs at the profitable Attorneys and Dentists headings. Just proceeding these headings are related Referral Services. Dentists and Attorneys sometimes advertise at this less active heading to gain positioning advantage over their colleagues. Care to guess to whom these "referral services" refer callers?

Recent complaints from advertisers hurt by heading jumpers have caused directory companies to crack down. Advertisers who appear to be heading jumping will sometimes be required to devote a substantial portion of their Display ad space to the subject of the heading they wish to advertise under. In this case, gaining a better position must be balanced against the potential loss if customers scan ads carefully.

To find out if heading jumping can benefit you, examine the headings just before your correct ones. This will tell you if heading jumping is a feasible move.

RATES: HOW THEY ARE DETERMINED

When a salesperson quotes a rate for an ad, the primary factor that decides this rate is distribution, or how many copies of the directory are circulated. The more directories a company must print and distribute, the greater its costs.

At the same time, the more directories that circulate, the greater the number of consumers who see your ad. This means more customer potential for you and tends to balance out the higher rates you pay for your advertising.

Businesses that draw customers from a wide area, such as movers or building contractors, usually complain less about high advertising rates than a business that gets its customers primarily from the neighborhood. A dry cleaner or a barber, even though their customers may come from within blocks of their locations, must still pay the higher rate if they advertise in a directory that is delivered far beyond the area where potential customers live.

Companies that produce neighborhood directories capitalize on this discontent by agreeing that local businesses are wasting money for the printing and delivery of directories to consumers who are unlikely ever to be their customers. Producers of wide-area or overlay directories argue the opposite. People are creatures of habit, they say. Even though they may be looking for a dry cleaner or a barber located nearby, they get accustomed to using a wide-area directory because it handles both their local and long-distance shopping needs. Consumers, they insist, prefer to use a larger directory because they like a wide selection of businesses to choose from.

Research shows that the size of a directory *is* important to consumers. Some prefer to use a large directory and others, a small one. Although no reliable statistics exist, larger directories seem to have an edge, particularly where businesses are concerned.

WHY RATES VARY FROM ONE DIRECTORY TO ANOTHER

One way that salespeople consistently mislead you is by encouraging you to advertise in a directory simply because it has low rates. What they neglect to mention is that it also has a low distribution. Since the number of consumers who see your advertising has a bearing on how much business you can hope to get, the relationship between ad rates and distribution totals is vital.

Ad rates must be compared to distribution figures to get a true picture of what you are paying. If you encounter different rates for the same sized ad—whether in competing directories covering the same area or in one company's directories in two different areas—check the distribution figures.

For instance, if an ad runs $200 a month in Directory A and $400 in Directory B but Directory B has a distribution ten times that of Directory A, you are receiving a very different value from each dollar you invest. Rates alone are meaningless unless viewed in the context of total distribution. The following table illustrates.

Calculating Your Directory Cost Per Copy

DIRECTORY	MONTHLY RATE	Divided by	DISTRIBUTION	Equals	Cost per Copy
A	$200	÷	3,000	=	7¢
B	$400	÷	30,000	=	1¢

Ad in Directory A is one-half the rate of Ad in Directory B
But your Cost Per Copy is almost 7 times higher

For Your Calculations

DIRECTORY	MONTHLY RATE	Divided by	DISTRIBUTION	Equals	Cost per Copy
		÷		=	
		÷		=	
		÷		=	
		÷		=	

INDEPENDENTS VS. TELEPHONE COMPANY RATES

Aside from the major role that distribution totals play in determining advertising rates, independent directories usually offer lower rates than telephone company affiliated directories. It is not that printing and publishing costs are lower for the independents. In fact, they often use the same printers and publishers that the telephone company affiliates do.

Here's the reason they can rate their ads lower and still leave themselves a generous profit margin: Companies that contract to publish the telephone company Yellow Pages, while affiliated with them, do not share the same pocketbook. They often must pay commissions of 50 percent or more to the telephone company for the privilege of getting access to their records. The independents avoid this middleman, preferring not to pay the prohibitive costs to buy listings from the telephone company, and obtain listing information in other ways. This enables them to save a bundle. A portion of this savings is reflected in their attractive lower rates.

The flip side of this coin, however, is that because independent directory companies use less reliable methods to obtain listings, their directories are often incomplete. Some consumers become frustrated when they cannot find a listing for a business they are trying to contact, and they stop using that directory.

NEGOTIATING RATES

Some advertisers believe that Yellow Pages rates are negotiable and that salespeople have the discretion to wheel and deal. For the most part, this is untrue. Rates for each item of advertising in each directory in the country are published in advance of directory sales in *Rates & Data,* a publication of The National Yellow Pages Service Association. (See page 40.) If a quoted rate is different from that published in *Rates & Data,* it may be due to a last-minute promotional or a directory boundary change which affects distribution totals. But any rate changes apply equally to all customers.

Occasionally, directory companies (usually independents) give their representatives some leeway in negotiating rates or in offering free items of advertising as an inducement to buy. But this is rare. If after a lengthy battle over rates your salesperson does not relent, you can trust that she is powerless to make any changes. If she could, she would, as she is as anxious to make the sale as you are to get a deal.

There have been times when rate increases have been waived for customers who refused to renew their advertising under any other circumstances. You might try refusing to renew your advertising unless you can get last year's rates. It's worth a try. If it fails, you can always back down and renew anyway.

PAYING FOR YELLOW PAGES ADVERTISING

Directory charges are figured on a monthly basis and are normally billed that way. If you advertise in the local telephone company directory, your monthly advertising charges will appear on your telephone bill. If you advertise in an independent directory or in one published by a telephone company outside your local area, you will receive a separate monthly statement of your advertising charges.

Some companies begin billing after a directory is distributed, but others may bill you months before the directory is published and delivered. A deposit of two or three months charges is sometimes required as advance payment, and this sum is applied against your total bill.

Companies that bill you after publication of the directory may find your credit wanting and ask you to pay some portion of the year's advertising charges in advance. In extreme cases, full payment may be required before your order is accepted.

Some headings are asking for this kind of treatment. If you advertise under a heading that has a statistical history of poor credit risks—such as "Massage"—be prepared to pay in full in advance. Other related headings may invite the same policy. Your salesperson will inform you if this applies to any of your headings.

If your cash flow permits, you may want to pay in full in advance when a directory company offers a discount—usually 10 percent—for doing so. However, paying by the month is more common.

BARGAINS: TAKING ADVANTAGE OF THEM

As a business located inside the boundaries of a directory, you are entitled to free regular listings in the white pages and at your primary heading in the yellow pages for each telephone number you have (rotary numbers excluded). You may also be entitled to more.

Unfortunately, your salesperson may be reluctant to mention free items, preferring to sell you something and make a commission than to give you something for free and make nothing. Make sure you ask what free items of advertising or promotional and discount programs are available. Fierce directory competition has lately resulted in a barrage of them.

FREEBIES, PROMOTIONALS AND DISCOUNTS

Listings and Trademarks. Some directory companies offer businesses unlimited free listings in the directory. Occasionally free trademarks are given as a promotional offering, particularly when a directory company must do something extra to meet their competition. These small ads with an eye-catching logo give you good visibility.

Buy One, Get One Free. There are "Buy one, get one free" programs that apply to both Incolumn and Display advertising. These and discounts on multiple Display ads present a real savings to businesses that must be visible at many headings.

Waived Artwork Charges. Some directory companies throw in costly artwork at no charge. To appreciate how much this can save you, call a graphic designer or an artist to learn what it would run to have a logo designed or an ad drawn.

Adjustments: If you are eligible for an adjustment because of an error in last year's ad, you may be able to be paid off in free or discounted ads in this year's directory.

Once you have learned about all the freebies, promotionals and discounts that you are eligible for, work them into your program where possible.

CO-OPTING: DO YOU QUALIFY?

If you purchase products from a national manufacturer, such as General Electric, RCA, or Westinghouse, you may be eligible to have some of your Yellow Pages advertising expense picked up by them. Many national manufacturers rebate a percentage of your purchases in the form of paying a portion of your Yellow Pages advertising. If you think you might be eligible, manufacturers provide their distributors with media packages to give to you that outline their advertising requirements and reimbursement plans. Since some of your purchase dollars are allocated for this purpose, take advantage of it—you're paying for it, anyway.

ARE YOU A NATIONAL ADVERTISER?

If the scope of your Yellow Pages advertising covers at least three states and 20 or more directories, you qualify as a national advertiser. This enables you to have an Authorized Selling Representative (ASR) handle your advertising, which will save you considerable time and trouble. Costs are picked up by the directory publishing companies. For more information, contact NYPSA (See page 40).

REMOTE CALL FORWARDING: A SHOESTRING BRANCH OFFICE

If you have determined that advertising your business in outlying areas will be profitable, be sure to use Remote Call Forwarding (RCF). It enables you to obtain a telephone number that is local to the area you are advertising in and have calls automatically forwarded to your actual location.

Using RCF to reach customers in outlying areas saves you more than just the expense of your ads. For obvious reasons, telephone shoppers prefer to call a local number. A non-local number in an ad often does not get good results.

The prime advantage of RCF is that it offers you growth potential without the usual costs. It also helps you to test new market areas very inexpensively and even to operate there when the volume of business does not warrant a full office operation.

Surprisingly, the cost of installing RCF is slight compared to its benefits. There is a reasonable one-time service connection charge, a monthly service charge (usually under $20), and the direct dial rate for each call that is forwarded. RCF is available in most major cities and can be arranged by calling the telephone company.

The power of RCF is illustrated by the experience of Gary Davis of Davis Electrical whose business was located in an industrial area. He used RCF to tap into a number of outlying, lucrative residential and commercial areas. His ads in one directory pulled extremely well, but in a second area, the same ad with similar positioning did not get good results.

The RCF number in his successful ad was recognizable by people in that area as local. The unsuccessful ad also had an RCF number, but it was a new exchange and was not easily recognized by the area's inhabitants as local. Davis arranged to get a more recognizable RCF number to put in his ad the following year. The results were satisfying, and this ad now draws more business for him than any other ad he runs.

THE TOLL-FREE 800 NUMBERS

You may want to go a step farther and order an 800 WATS line. This allows free calling from a much wider area and is appropriate if you want to offer no charge calling to your customers, wherever they are. The telephone company can give you additional information about the installation of an 800 number.

DISTRIBUTION: HOW IT AFFECTS DIRECTORY USAGE

If a directory gets into the hands of consumers it will be used, while a free ad in a directory that is not distributed is no bargain. But how can you be sure that a directory is distributed?

For the most part, directories are delivered simply because to do so is in the best interests of directory companies. If they do not deliver their directories, they are guaranteeing that their advertisers will not get results during the year. While directory companies know that most advertisers do not survey their customers and will not know how their ads worked, some do check and will refuse to renew their advertising again.

Directory companies that claim 100 percent saturation delivery in a marketplace are stretching the truth. For the most part, directory companies farm out this uninteresting task to independent companies. They, in turn, employ unskilled labor whose major virtue is their possession of an automobile and well-developed arm muscles, useful in lifting heavy loads of books. These individuals are assigned streets and then hand deliver the directories to their destinations. Field inspectors conduct follow up spot checks, both in person and by telephone, in an effort to ensure that the books reach their destinations.

Nevertheless, reports come in of hundreds of directories sitting in back alley dumpsters. These are usually extras rather than an indication that consumers are without their copies. Where the Public Utilities Commission once regulated Yellow Pages advertising, higher rates could only be justified by increased distribution figures. As a result, these figures were often overstated, and many more directories were printed than necessary. In a rare case, a tired deliverer may have seen a quick way to finish his day's labor, but the system of checks by supervisors keeps this practice to a minimum.

Independent directory companies estimate their distribution by the number of addresses rather than by the number of telephones, and this can account for differences in distribution figures between directories covering the same geographical area.

Always ask for distribution figures in printed form. Verbal estimates are worthless. Salespeople have been heard to quote a distribution figure to be ten times that of what it really is.

The month during which a directory is published and delivered may be critical to your success. If your business is seasonal or highly dependent on Christmas trade, for example, advertising in a directory that is distributed in November may be more profitable than one with a January distribution since a directory experiences its peak usage just after delivery. New businesses should be very concerned with distribution dates. They need exposure as soon as possible, so the earlier the directory is delivered, the better.

"I DIDN'T GET A DIRECTORY"

Often an advertiser claims that he didn't receive a directory. Just as often, a quick look on the shelf or in a desk drawer produces it. If not, a telephone call to the distribution center can determine the exact date and time of delivery as well as the homes and businesses on that block that were premise or phone checked to confirm delivery to that street. If he still insists he did not receive a directory, and homes or businesses on his street have theirs, it is safe to conclude that a copy was delivered but was later tossed away or removed.

Of course, directory companies cannot take responsibility for directories once they have been delivered. While it is not impossible that a vicious dog or a closed business prevented delivery, these cases are infrequent.

The fact that most directory companies deliver their directories was demonstrated to me on one occasion when I was trying to sell an ad to a printer. He agreed to buy advertising, but wanted to use the same ad he was currently running in a local independent. He couldn't find his copy and I was unable to produce it from the collection in the trunk of my car, so I went in search of it on the block. In the course of going door to door on this main thoroughfare, I discovered something very interesting.

Of the five directories that were distributed in this area—call them directories A through E—I found not one business that had all five. Some had A and B. Others had C and D. Others had A, C and E. Common sense dictates that the directories were not delivered in this erratic fashion. It is more reasonable to assume that all the directories were delivered and that the missing ones had been carried off, thrown away or misplaced.

DISTRIBUTION TO NEWCOMERS

Newcomers to an area represent an excellent source of income to you because people new to an area have so many needs to fill and have not yet established the habit of doing business with any one in particular.

Most newcomers to an area can get a Yellow Pages directory at the telephone company office when they drop by to pick up their telephones. If they already have their telephones, they may not need to go to the business office and then become dependent on the telephone company delivering a copy of the directory to them.

Telephone companies have the advantage of knowing about all new telephone installations and can easily arrange delivery of a directory if they want to. Sometimes they do and sometimes they don't. Independents, on the other hand, do not have access to records of new telephone installations. If they want to provide directories to newcomers to an area, they must find out about them in another way.

Some independent companies do a secondary delivery to all businesses half way through the year. Others provide secondary delivery by purchasing mailing lists from companies that keep track of real estate transactions and business license transfers by zip code.

This, of course, offers them no information on new apartment tenants, and this is often where the majority of newcomers reside. Yellow Pages salespeople will tell you that extra copies of directories are left with apartment managers to dole out to newcomers, but in fact this is rarely done. If it is, there is no way to tell if these directories ever reach the newcomers since it is left entirely to the discretion of an unmotivated party. On the other hand, telephone directories are usually not removed by vacating apartment dwellers as they are in the more thorough cleanup done in sold homes and businesses, so this may not be an important issue.

BEWARE OF MAIL SOLICITATIONS!

Speaking of distribution, be wary of solicitations for directory advertising that arrive in the mail. This scam is an outgrowth of the easily recognized Yellow Pages. On a postcard size solicitation bearing the walking fingers logo, it will state in barely legible type, "THIS IS NOT A BILL." The scammers are banking on the fact that that will be precisely what you think it is and that you will pay it.

In fact, it is a request that you send a sum of money—around $100—to provide you with a listing in a Yellow Pages directory. Many already confused business owners think it is a solicitation for advertising in yet another directory local to their area, and they remit the fee. They fail, however, to read the fine print which states that distribution of the directory is left to the discretion of the publisher. The fact is they have no obligation to distribute any copies at all. And they usually don't.

Chapter Three

WHAT
YOU NEED TO KNOW
ABOUT YOUR OWN
BUSINESS

"ADVERTISING DOESN'T COST, IT PAYS"

If advertising is working, it doesn't cost, it pays. If your monthly rate for Yellow Pages advertising is $100 and your ad brings in customers who spend $1,000, your advertising has cost you nothing. What's more, you are ahead by $900, much of which you might have lost if you did not have the advertising.

Unfortunately, for a lack of knowledge on the part of business owners, advertising in the Yellow Pages may not work—or work as well as it might. And $100 worth of advertising that brings you no return has cost you $100. Not only that, but you have lost an unknown amount of money that could have been yours if your advertising had worked.

Cost-effective advertising means that money you invest is justified by the return you get. It is generally measured by the ratio of profit to cost. This makes it essential that you know exactly what your costs and profits are.

An ad is minimally cost-effective if it brings in enough business to pay for itself. But breaking even is not what most people have in mind when they advertise in the Yellow Pages. They want to make a profit on their investment — and the bigger, the better.

How to determine your advertising profits is covered in Chapter Five, which details how to check the results of your ads and to act on them. Now you're going to calculate your advertising costs by applying THE WAGNER YELLOW PAGES PROFIT FORMULA. This is the key to matching your business's needs to what the Yellow Pages can offer.

THE WAGNER YELLOW PAGES PROFIT FORMULA

THE WAGNER YELLOW PAGES PROFIT FORMULA has two components — Cost Per Customer (CPC) and Average Customer Worth (ACW). You'll soon see why you need these two.

Rate vs. Cost. Most advertisers make the mistake of confusing the term *"rate"* with the term *"cost."* But you need to know right now that your monthly advertising rate is not your actual cost.

We have already looked at one factor that interferes with rate and cost meaning the same — distribution figures. Unless a monthly rate is divided by distribution totals, it cannot be meaningfully compared to another rate, and your true cost remains unknown.

An ad in Directory "A" at $75 per month may seem less costly than the same sized Ad in Directory "B" at $225 per month. But if Directory "A" has a distribution of 50,000 copies and Directory "B," a distribution of 500,000 copies, which costs more? The ad in Directory "B" may have a monthly rate three times that of the ad in Directory "A," but if your advertising is seen by ten times the number of people, your potential for business is ten times greater and your advertising is less costly.

Forget the monthly rate as an indicator of your actual cost. Instead, to learn your real costs, look at the two components of THE WAGNER YELLOW PAGES PROFIT FORMULA — Cost Per Customer (CPC) and Average Customer Worth (ACW). They will tell you what your advertising costs really are, and costs go well beyond what your monthly rates are.

COST PER CUSTOMER (CPC).

Cost per customer means how much it costs you to make a customer of someone. If a $100 monthly ad brings you 2 customers, your CPC is $50 ($100 divided by 2). If a $200 ad brings you 10 customers, then your CPC is $20 ($200 divided by 10).

Many advertisers think they are saving money when they buy a small ad instead of a large one, but research indicates that larger ads bring in more customers. The rate for a larger ad may run as much as 6 or 8 times that of a smaller ad, but it can pull in 15 times as many customers. This means a small ad has a higher Cost Per Customer, and while it has a lower rate, it actually costs you more than a larger ad.

The CPC factor becomes most critical at a highly competitive heading, where the size of an ad profoundly affects both (1) your position among all Display ads at the heading, and (2) your distance from the start of the heading. At a less active heading, your ad size will also affect your position, but it hurts you less because your ad will not be so far from the start of the heading that shoppers are likely to overlook it.

Because of this, the more competitive your heading, the higher your Cost Per Customer with a smaller ad. At less competitive headings, the difference in CPC between the largest and smallest ads is reduced.

When deciding what size ad to buy, your decision must be based on the amount of activity at your headings. The more activity, the lower your actual cost for a larger ad, no matter what the rate is. A smaller ad actually costs more as your Cost Per Customer is higher.

AVERAGE CUSTOMER WORTH (ACW).

If you add up how much money your business took in last year and divide that amount by the number of customer transactions you had, you will know how much your average customer is worth. Your Average Customer Worth (ACW) is a critical factor in determining how heavy a weight monthly rate should have in deciding how much to spend in the Yellow Pages.

If you cannot estimate your ACW, total the number of invoices from last year and divide this number into your net profit. For example, if your net profit last year was $100,000 and you carried out 1,000 transactions, then your average customer worth is $100 ($100,000 divided by 100). If you had

10 transactions, your average customer worth is $10,000 ($100,000 divided by 10).

Now let's look at both of these again and put them together.

CPC is your monthly advertising rate divided by the number of customers your ad yields.

ACW is how much your average customer nets you.

Make sure that you understand these concepts. They are the basis for the many decisions you will have to make about Yellow Pages advertising.

CPC is an excellent tool for finding out the real cost of your advertising — whether you are comparing rates for different advertising media, ads in competing Yellow Pages directories, or two different sized ads in the same directory.

For example, let's say that Ad A is $300 a month and Ad B is $100 per month. After your ad results are in, you discover that the returns on these ads are different. Or perhaps you have yet to advertise, but want to figure your potential profits ahead of time using rates and projected profits provided to you by different advertising media representatives. Your calculations might look like this.

AD	RATE	CUSTOMERS PRODUCED	COST PER CUSTOMER
A	$300	20	$15
B	$100	10	$10

In this case, even though Ad A brings in twice as many customers as Ad B, the CPC for AD B is less since it has cost less to get each customer. Ad B is therefore more cost effective.

Now add the ACW factor to this calculation.

If Average Customer Worth (ACW) is $40:

AD	CUSTOMERS PRODUCED	ACW	INCOME	AD RATE	NET PROFIT
A	20	x $40	= $800	- $300	= $500
B	10	x $40	= $400	- $100	= $300

As you can see, CPC is less for Ad B, but Ad A results in higher profits because it brought in more customers. As ACW increases, this becomes even more pronounced. For example, consider the cases where ACW is first $100 and then $500.

AD	CUSTOMERS PRODUCED	ACW	INCOME	AD RATE	NET PROFIT
A	20	x $100	= $2,000	- $300	= $1,700
B	10	x $100	= $1,000	- $100	= $ 900
A	20	x $500	= $10,000	- $300	= $9,700
B	10	x $500	= $ 5,000	- $100	= $4,900

As you can see, the higher your Average Customer Worth, the less important Cost Per Customer becomes. Generating the greatest number of customers overrides how much it costs you to get a customer since each is worth so much to you. Further, you need so few customers to pay for your advertising.

Now look at the effect on your cost if you have a relatively low ACW. Let's take the cases where ACW is first $15 and then $10.

Worth Remembering

The cost of your ads in the Yellow Pages is not the rate you pay for them.

AD	CUSTOMERS PRODUCED	ACW	INCOME	AD RATE	NET PROFIT
A	20	x $15	= $300	- $300	= 0
B	10	x $15	= $150	- $100	= $50
A	20	x $10	= $200	- $300	= ($100)
B	10	x $10	= $100	- $100	= 0

As you can see, when your ACW is low, ad rates become a critical factor in whether your Yellow Pages program will turn a profit for you. In this case, the ad with the lower rate has resulted in your making a profit or breaking even while in the case of the ad with the higher rate, you could even suffer a loss.

The WAGNER YELLOW PAGES PROFIT FORMULA uses CPC and ACW to determine how much your Yellow Pages advertising is really costing.

CPC is useful when comparing different advertising media, different directories or different sized ads. You might be deciding whether the Yellow Pages, the newspaper or direct mail is more cost-effective for your advertising campaign. Or you might be comparing the real costs of ads — whether in the same directory or in competing directories. CPC gives you a tool for comparing, while rate alone tells you little.

ACW lets you know how beneficial it is for you to buy larger ads to maximize the number of customers you draw.

IF YOU HAVE A LARGE ACW: You can be less concerned about ad rates since even one customer can make a tremendous difference in your profit.

IF YOU HAVE A SMALL ACW: Unless you expect to draw great hordes of customers, monthly rate matters greatly as it can make the difference in whether your advertising is a moneymaker or simply another addition to your operating expenses.

Your ACW also tells you how many customers you need to pay for your advertising. For example, an attorney whose ACW is $8,000 needs only one customer during the year to pay for his

$6,000 program. A dry cleaner, whose average customer may only be worth $20, needs 300 customers a year to pay for the identical program. Here's a worksheet for you to use to figure out your own CPC and ACW.

CALCULATING YOUR ACW		
Income 19 ———	÷ Number of Customer Transactions	= Worth of Average Customer

CALCULATING YOUR CPC		
Monthly Rate of Ad	÷ Number of Customers Ad Brought In	= Your Cost Per Customer

Now you have some idea of how much advertising you can afford, so let's move on to another level of detail.

PHYSICAL PREPARATION. Your physical preparation revolves around learning as much as possible about the three elements that are at the core of your Yellow Pages program:

(1) What size ads you need

(2) Whether you stand to gain from advertising in directories in outlying areas

(3) What headings you must be represented under.

Sit down with pencil and paper and all the directories that cover your local area. If you are not sure what these directories are, ask an advertising plumber. Every Yellow Pages salesperson within a 50 mile radius has beaten a track to a plumber's door at one time or another. He will know the directories that apply and be able to tell you what they are.

WHAT SIZE ADS DO YOU NEED?

How much do you know about your business? If you have been in business for a while, you probably know quite a bit. If this is a new venture for you, however, you need to learn a few things about the relationship between your business and the Yellow Pages.

The best way to accomplish this is to open the Yellow Pages to your major heading. The number of ads and their sizes will give you an idea of how aggressive you must be to compete. Use the following rules to help you decide:

Worth Remembering

Compare ad rates by how much you pay for each directory that is distributed. Divide the rate by the number of directories circulated to give you a cost per copy figure.

RULE #1 *The more ads there are at a heading, the more important the size of your ad.* This is true because many ads at a heading push a small ad way back. It gets fewer responses, and this increases your Cost Per Customer (CPC).

RULE #2 *The fewer the ads at a heading, the less important the size of your ad.* In this case, CPC will not vary so much from one size ad to another.

RULE #3 *If the few ads are all large ones, to compete you will need a large ad.* Surveys show that people tend to associate larger ads with credibility and reliability. A small ad at a heading with mostly large ones will be sending a boy to do a man's job.

RULE #4 *If there are many ads but they are all small, it means that your ad can be small too and still be competitive.* It also means that you might consider buying a bigger ad in order to dominate the heading, or to use red ink to make your ad stand out.

RULE #5 *If your business has more than one location, a large ad is warranted.* The cost of the ad can be split several ways, and you get the benefits of good positioning and low cost per location.

RULE #6 *New businesses must be particularly aggressive.* They do not yet have an established customer base to fall back on. Over one-half of new businesses fail before the first year is up. This chilling fact, plus the reputation the Yellow Pages has for bringing in new customers, underlines the importance of visibility in the Yellow Pages for new businesses if they plan to beat the odds.

SHOULD YOU ADVERTISE IN OUTLYING DIRECTORIES?

The decision to advertise in directories in outlying areas in addition to those that cover your local area rests on your answers to the following questions:

(1) Are you the type of business that goes to the customer, such as a carpet cleaner or a building contractor?

(2) How wide an area do you serve now? If you already have trucks handling customers in an outlying area, would more customers there keep your trucks busy and cut your costs?

(3) How wide an area can you serve? There are increased costs associated with traveling greater distances to service customers. How far can you travel and still remain profitable?

(4) Have you saturated the local market, creating a need to draw customers from other areas?

(5) If you have the type of business where your customers come to you, such as an auto dealership or a furniture store, how far will customers travel to get to you?

(6) Do you deal in a high-ticket, infrequently purchased item so that consumers will not mind traveling a distance to save money?

(7) Do you offer something special, such as hard-to-find items or an unusual brand, that will make it necessary for people to travel to get what they want?

(8) Do you provide unique services, such as staying open seven days, when businesses of your type usually do not?

(9) Is your business located in a declining area so that you are forced to pull business from outlying growth areas with higher-income populations?

(10) Is your business located where two or more directories meet so that your local market overlaps several publications?

(11) Does your reputation stretch far and wide so that customers from far distances are likely to have heard of you and want to deal with you?

(12) Are businesses of your type spread so far apart that customers must travel to you even if you are located at a considerable distance from them?

If you answer "Yes" to any of these questions, you may be a good candidate to reap profits from advertising in outlying directories.

For further tips, read the content of the ads at your headings to see from how far a distance your competition is advertising. If all the advertising at your heading is local, your type of business probably draws mostly from the local marketplace, and advertising in adjacent directories will not be profitable.

If many businesses from outside your area are advertising at the heading, then you must consider adjacent markets. They represent good business for you, business that you will need to make up for local customers lost to your distant advertising competitors. You can usually tell businesses from outside the local area by their addresses. Unfortunately, distant businesses sometimes omit their addresses for precisely the reason that they wish to appear local.

WHAT HEADINGS SHOULD YOU BE UNDER?

An average Yellow Pages directory offers over 5,000 headings that are fairly consistent from one directory to another. In some cases, the wording of a heading may vary slightly or some directory companies will offer headings that others do not.

All 5,000 headings will not necessarily appear in every Yellow Pages directory because a heading is omitted when no one wants to list under it. Even if a heading does not appear in a directory, it is still available. Yellow Pages salespeople normally carry a complete list of all headings. If you cannot find one you want, ask to see this list.

Most businesses sell more than one product or offer more than one service. Since there is no way to know exactly which headings consumers will look under when ready to buy, you can hedge your bet by being visible under as many headings as possible. Of course, it is not necessary to do extensive advertising at each of these headings. Often a listing will do the job.

Advertisers sometimes complain that there are too many similar headings, forcing them to increase their monthly advertising expense for the sake of being represented at all of them. To illustrate this dilemma, imagine that Mrs. Jones can no longer care for her aged mother and must find a place to house her. Which heading will she look under — Nursing Homes, Rest Homes, Residential Care, Sanitariums, or Convalescent Homes?

If Mr. Brown, a do-it-yourselfer, wants to buy tools and supplies to construct a deck in his backyard, which heading will he choose — Building Materials, Tools, Hardware Stores, or Lumber?

The Smiths are ready to have dinner and want to order some Italian food to take out. Which heading will they select — Pizzas, Restaurants, or Foods-Carry out?

The number of headings that apply to any particular business can vary, but the more hooks you throw out, the greater the chance you will catch a fish. People who use the Yellow Pages are ready to buy. There is nothing saved by losing a new customer or an old and favored one to a competitor simply because you cannot be found at a heading.

A prepared salesperson will be able to inform you of all headings related to your business since this is one way in which he hopes to increase the amount of advertising he sells to you. On the other hand, you can't depend on this because he may be inexperienced or hurried. If you are not familiar with all the headings that apply to your business, your salesperson carries a list of every imaginable product and service with all related headings. Ask to see it.

It is also worth your time to itemize every product and service you offer and consult the Index in the Yellow Pages for appropriate headings. Also helpful is to ask friends and associates where in the Yellow Pages they would look for what you sell.

Consider how much profit you make from a particular product or service when you are deciding whether or not to advertise it under an additional heading. When you consider the yearly rate for a bold listing or a small Incolumn ad and how few customers you would need to pay for it, your attitude about advertising at additional headings should change.

Knowing which headings to advertise under is also made easier when you see which your competitors have chosen. If you intend to give them a run for their money, you should at least have minimal representation where they do.

In a rare case you may simply not be able to find an appropriate heading under which to list one of your products or services. Headings are continually being modified and updated, but this process is a step or two behind. In the meantime, advertising at an inappropriate heading might result in a potential customer having trouble finding you.

You will remember the case of Bill Dugan of T-Tops Unlimited with which this book began. Bill's problem was that there was no heading for T-Tops, which was what he sold. An inexperienced salesperson had put his ad at "Automobile Sunroofs," where no one thought to look for T-Tops.

A disaster like Bill's is easily remedied. If you see the potential to make money at a heading that does not exist, request it. It may take time to arrange, but it will be well worth it. If the heading request is denied, ask for a Heading Cross-Reference instead. This is easily inserted and refers shoppers to a related heading where you are advertising. You keep your customers and protect your investment.

Bill tried that the next year. His heading request for T-Tops was denied, but he was able to get a Heading Cross-Reference at T-Tops that referred customers to the heading where his ad was. Bill had a very different experience with Yellow Pages the second year he tried it. It paid off.

By scrutinizing the content of the ads at your headings, you will find clues to other appropriate headings. For each service and product mentioned, look in the Index to see if a heading exists. If so, are your competitors advertising here? To what extent? Answers to these questions will help you decide if you need representation at the heading just to compete and how aggressive you must be. You may elect to do minor advertising, such as a bold listing, even if your competition is doing little or nothing. This would make sense, particularly if your product or service is very profitable.

There is no harm in being one of the only ads at a heading. This means little competition, and consumers will be likely to call you when they consult this heading. Ordering an ad that is just a bit larger than the largest already at the heading will result in good positioning, and your ad will attract the most attention when shoppers look there.

THE SPECIALITY GUIDES

Speciality Guides follow a heading and break a type of business into its specialties. Examples of headings that have speciality guides following them are Attorneys, Dentists, and Restaurants. In some areas, Pharmacies and other headings are followed by a Specialty Guide that breaks these businesses down by location for the shopper's convenience. Don't overlook the Specialty Guides as a source of customers.

Someone seeking an attorney who specializes in real estate law or a dentist who is experienced in working on children may go directly to the Specialty Guide. People interested in dining out at a Mexican Restaurant may accidentally come upon the Restaurant Specialty Guide and select their restaurant from there. Some directory companies offer unlimited free light-type listings to their advertisers, and the Specialty Guides are one place you want to take advantage of this, unless more aggressive advertising is called for.

Worth Remembering

Consumers may go directly to the Specialty Guide, bypassing the general heading. If your heading is followed by a Specialty Guide, use it to advertise your specialty products and services.

R Restaurants 806

Guide to RESTAURANTS

Specialties listed by type of cuisine.

Restaurants, Sandwiches (Cont'd)

TRANSPORTATION SANDWICH SHOP
SANDWICHES - BREAKFAST
ACROSS FROM THE OLD MARRIOTT
SERVING FROM 7AM - 4PM
3802) 297th Pl SE ----------- 825-6342

TUCKER CAFE
SERVING LUNCH FROM 11:00-2:30
MON-FRI. LOC. IN THE
TUCKER SHOPPING CENTER
1418 Talbot Rd S----------226-7920

WAGON WHEEL THE
GOOD HOME STYLE COOKING
AT AN AFFORDABLE PRICE
OPEN M-F 6-5
526 S 2d ---------------226-4423

Restaurants, Seafood

BONE'S STEAK AND SEAFOOD
SERVING STEAKS AND SEAFOOD
OPEN 7 DAYS A WEEK
22245 104th Pl SE ------------ 852-6165

Boston Sea Party
25829 104th SE ------------ 854-7084

BUCKHEAD BISTRO
WE SERVE SOME OF THE FINEST
SEAFOOD IN TOWN
OPEN LATE NIGHT UNTIL 4:00 AM
327 S Central ----------------- 852-2174

CAMPBELL & CO'S STEAMBOAT BAY
FEATURING STEAMED SEAFOOD
CAJUN STYLE BLACKEN REDFISH
FABULOUS BUFFALO WINGS
909 N Bdway ----------------- 288-6688

Captain Billy's Fish House
257-1/2 E Main ------------- 939-2920
Captain D's Seafood Restaurants
91 Buford Hwy Ne
CARAVAN'S CRAB SHACK
61 Memo

Restaurants, Seafood (Cont'd)

J D DEMPSEY'S
Great Food At Reasonable Prices
19005 64th S Kent------------------- 251-9688
Jim White Half Shell Restaurant
271 Rainier N ------------------ 226-2965
JOHN'S SEAFOOD
29630 Green River Rd SE ----------- 833-2350

L & N SEAFOOD GRILL
FRESH SEAFOOD GRILLED OVER A
MESQUITE GRILL • OPEN FOR LUNCH &
DINNER & SUNDAY BRUNCH
34233 Pacific Hy S FedWy---------838-4707

LONG JOHN SILVER SEAFOOD SHOP
Wide Variety Of Seafood
Fried Fish - Clams
Battered Shrimps
1807 S 223d ----------------824-2080

MARKET CAFE AND SEAFOOD BAR
SERVING DELICIOUS STEAKS
AND SEAFOOD 7 DAYS A WEEK
325 Burnett N --------------------255-1453

MARRA'S A SEAFOOD GRILL
FRESH GRILLED SEAFOODS
OPEN FOR LUNCH FROM 11:30-2:30 &
DINNER 6:00-11:00 PM
100 S Southwest ------------------939-3971

MEXICO CITY GOURMET
SOME OF THE BEST AUTHENTIC MEXICAN
CUISINE FOUND IN THE SOUTH
DISHES FROM ALL OVER MEXICO
2407 M Southeast ----------------833-3827

MICHAEL'S RESTAURANT & LOUNGE
SERVING STEAKS, SEAFOOD
AND A WHOLE LOT MORE
OPEN MON-FRI 11:30-10:
410 Raylor D

111

WHICH BUSINESSES PROFIT MOST FROM THE YELLOW PAGES?

Businesses experience different degrees of success when they advertise in the Yellow Pages. Of all businesses in an area, directory companies recognize that only half will be good candidates to buy advertising in the Yellow Pages. And only half of these will be motivated by past experience to spend any substantial amount. Here's how you can find out how much you stand to gain from Yellow Pages advertising.

Pick up a directory and look up the heading, "Plumbing Contractors." Compare the activity there to that at "Investment Management." You are looking at the difference between high and low potential headings.

Now grab a handful of Yellow Pages directories and look up the headings that apply to your business. If they are brimming over with ads, your chances of doing well are excellent. On the other hand, finding little activity at your headings does not mean that you have nothing to gain from Yellow Pages advertising. Aside from drumming up customers, the Yellow Pages serves other functions, such as presenting an image, being a memory jogger to a forgetful customer, or establishing your credibility. Low activity at your heading, however, is a hint that you will need to resort to other means to get most of your customers.

When consumers were asked which headings they looked up most often, their answers looked like this.

Worth Remembering

If you can't find a heading that fits what you sell or do, ask for it. If you're turned down, request a Heading Cross-Reference.

Headings Looked Up Most Often

By Businesses	Order	By Residences
Plumbing Contractors	1	Cleaners
Lumber — Retail	2	Physicians & Surgeons (M.D.)
Automobile Parts — Retail	3	Department Stores
Electric Contractors	4	Television Dealers & Services
Signs	5	Taxicabs
Physicians & Surgeons (M.D.)	6	Beauty Shops
Television Dealers & Services	7	Air Conditioning Contr & Svc
Hardware — Retail	8	Washing Machines & Dryers
Automobile Dealers — New Cars	9	Lumber — Retail
Paper & Paper Products	10	Plumbing Contractors
Automobile Parts — Wholesale	11	Refrigerators & Freezers–Dlrs & Svc
Restaurants	12	Furniture Dealers — Retail
Refrigerators & Freezers — Dlrs & Svc	13	Dentists
Service Stations	14	Florists — Retail
Paint — Retail	15	Hardware — Retail
Glass — Auto, Plate, Window, etc.	16	Oils — Fuel
Printers	17	Bakeries — Retail
Automobile Repairing & Service	18	Hospitals, Clinics
Office Equipment & Supplies	19	Electric Appliance Dealers
Roofing Contractors	20	Grocers — Retail
Air Conditioning Contr & Svc	21	Laundries
General Contractors	22	Paint — Retail
Tire Dealers — Retail	23	Pharmacies
Taxicabs	24	Carpet & Rug Cleaners
Florists — Retail	25	Automobile Dealers — New Cars
Grocers — Wholesale	26	Service Stations
Steel & Steel Products	27	Restaurants
Trucking	28	Upholsterers
Oils — Fuel	29	Gas Liquefied
Cleaners	30	Vacuum Cleaners — Dlrs & Svc
Beer and Liquor	31	Real Estate
Refrigeration Equipment — Comm	32	Shoes — Retail
Electric Motors — Dlrs & Svc	33	Automobile Repairing
Washing Machines & Dryers	34	Furnaces — Dealers & Service
Travel Agents	35	Lawn Mowers
Beauty & Barber Shop—Equip & Supp	36	General Contractors
Furnaces — Dealers & Service	37	Insurance
Meat — Wholesale	38	Ranges & Stoves
Insurance	39	Schools & Universities
Painting Contractors	40	Draperies
Building Materials	41	Painting Contractors
Typewriters — Dealers & Service	42	Electric Contractors
Plumbing & Heating Supplies—Retail	43	Sporting Goods
Attorneys	44	Heating Contractors
Beauty Shops	45	Sewer & Septic Contr & Clnrs
Real Estate	46	Automobile Parts — Retail
Stationers — Retail	47	Towing Automotive
Rental Service Stores	48	Attorneys
Electric Appliance Dealers	49	Travel Agents
Welding	50	Concrete Constr Materials

If your business does not appear on this list, don't despair. Look up your headings and see how many ads there are. With over 5,000 headings in the Yellow Pages, being in the top 50 is not critical to profitable advertising.

As you can see, service businesses do very well from the Yellow Pages. Other big winners are businesses often shopped by telephone, such as hardware stores that people call in search of a particular item, or travel agents who can arrange tickets by telephone. Businesses that require an appointment, such as an attorney, a dentist, or a beauty salon, or that take reservations, such as restaurants, are sure moneymakers from the Yellow Pages. If your business offers delivery or pickup, such as florists, auto-towing services or taxicab companies, Yellow Pages advertising is a good bet.

If your business caters to emergency situations, you are a natural to profit from the Yellow Pages. Some businesses that deal with emergency buyers are obvious, such as plumbers, locksmiths, electricians, or appliance repair services. But if you think about it, almost every business has its emergency market. A woman who tears her dress hours before she is due at a business meeting is a tailor's emergency buyer. Someone throwing a last-minute party is a liquor store's emergency customer. A careless spill on the rug before company is expected is an emergency for the carpet cleaner. Consider the ways in which your business might capitalize on these situations, particularly if in your ad you mention your willingness to give quick service on such occasions.

CONTRACTORS: A SPECIAL TIP

If the Yellow Pages were designed for any one business, it would have to be for contractors. Contractors spend more money on Yellow Pages advertising than any other class of business, and for good reason: they generally make the most money from their investment. If you are an advertising contractor who is not making money, something is terribly wrong. Small fortunes are made each year by contractors with Yellow Pages advertising, even when they run only Incolumn ads.

This book tells you how to correct many of the things that prevent a business from profiting from the Yellow Pages. But it is a safe bet that if you are not making money, you may be your own worst enemy.

Consumers frequently complain about contractors, and their complaints can be summarized in one word: Unreliable. They claim contractors don't return calls and don't show up when they say they will. If you are a contractor and this applies to you, even a small ad in the Yellow Pages will be profitable for your business if you change your tactics and deal with potential customers in a responsible manner.

Overcome with frustration, more and more consumers are asking friends or neighbors for the name of a reliable contractor. If you get a reputation as one, your Yellow Pages results will be even more impressive as one call leads to a host of referrals.

UPDATING ADVERTISING TO REFLECT CHANGES IN YOUR BUSINESS

During the year your business may have undergone a number of changes, or you may plan some modifications in the near future. These may range from changing the name of your business to a willingness to give free estimates to putting in a new line of products. Your salesperson is not a mind reader. It is up to you to make sure that these changes are reflected in your advertising.

Answer the following questions before you say, "Leave it the same."

Have you changed your business name, address, or telephone number?

Have you added a telephone number?

Have you changed your logo or slogan?

Do you want to tie in to your Yellow Pages advertising any other advertising you may be doing?

If your years in business are included in your ad, have you updated them by one?

Have you added or deleted any changes in authorized brand names for sales or service?

Have you updated information on licenses, bonds, or insurance?

Do you still handle only retail?

Do you still cater only to the residential trade?

Has your variety and selection changed? If so, how?

Do you still service the same market areas?

Are you now offering pickup or delivery?

Have your business hours or days remained the same?

Do you now take credit cards? Which ones?

Do you give estimates?

Have your parking facilities changed?

Have you added or changed illustrations?

Has your location remained the same? Is it appropriate to add a map or landmark to your ads?

Has any emphasis changed on products or services in terms of profit potential?

Have you increased or decreased your capacity to service the public?

Until you answer these questions and others like them that you can think of, you shouldn't be finalizing your advertising! Think again about the directories you are advertising in, the headings you are represented under, and the ad sizes you have. Look carefully at your ad copy which may require changes. Go through the worksheets, guides and checklists in this section to make sure your business really is the same as it was a year ago. You'll be surprised at what you find.

Chapter Four

HOW TO DEAL WITH SALESPEOPLE AND WHAT TO WATCH OUT FOR

HOW CONTACT IS MADE

Only one-half the businesses in an area will have any contact with a Yellow Pages salesperson, and half of these will be limited to a telephone call.

If you are currently an advertiser, your account will be assigned to a salesperson who will either drop in at your store or call beforehand to make an appointment. It is unlikely that you will be overlooked because salespeople know their best bets for a sale are current advertisers. Nonetheless, accounts do get lost in the system. You do not want this to happen to you, whether you plan to keep the advertising as it is, make changes, or cancel it. Make a note to call the directory company if you have not been contacted by their representative at least four months before the directory's publication date.

If you are not currently advertising, the chances of being overlooked increase. You may be part of the 50 percent of businesses that are either not contacted or only telephoned because you are considered low potential to buy. Or your business may be assigned to a salesperson who will, herself, judge it too low in potential to merit contact. If you do not receive a visit or a telephone call from a salesperson at least four months before a directory is scheduled to be published, take the bull by the horns and call the company to initiate contact.

If you are a new business, particularly one that operates from a residence, the chances of being overlooked increase. Call the company if you want to advertise or simply want information. You can usually count on a telephone call bringing someone to your door promptly. Customers that initiate contact with Yellow Pages salespeople are called "kiss-me's" or "laydowns" and are highly coveted by the salesforce.

MEETING WITH A SALESPERSON

When a sharp Yellow Pages salesperson calls on you, she will already have in hand some information on your business, including your name, address and telephone number and additional telephone numbers and locations you have. She will have cut out your current ads and checked your headings for positioning and competition. She will also have checked all related headings and directories from outlying areas and know your programs there and what you are paying for them.

She will know something about your business, either through experience or research. She may already have dropped by your location to pick up your business card and to get a feel for your layout and stock. If you are not currently advertising, she will have prepared ads for you. If you are, she will have analyzed your existing ads and prepared others if they seem ineffective or flat. If you are a current advertiser, she will know your paying habits. If you owe any money for previous advertising, she will know how much and try to collect it.

On the basis of all this, she may have designed a program that she feels will benefit both of you. She has considered your potential objections and has the answers to them. If she suspects cost will be an obstacle, she may suggest ways to trim unnecessary dollars that you are spending to advertise with other directory companies and then attempt to persuade you to spend those "saved" dollars with her. Analyze her suggestions carefully. Perhaps you *were* oversold last year. On the other hand, she may just be chopping arbitrarily, and this could hurt you.

If she suspects she may have to persuade you, she will be loaded down with materials to support the credibility of her company. She will have surveys and testimonial letters on hand to use in convincing you that her directory is the best.

Not every Yellow Pages salesperson, however, will take all these measures. She may be new to the business and not have information about competing directories to bring to bear on the situation. She may have overslept and missed the last sales meeting where new promotional programs that might benefit you were discussed. She may know about them but try to sell you something else that will make her more money. She may not mention free items of advertising that you are entitled to, hoping instead to sell you something that will bring her a commission. She may simply not care about you or your business. Worse yet, she may be dishonest.

This is where chapters two and three of this book pay off. If you have done your preparation, whether or not she has, you will be capable of arranging an advertising program that will bring you the customers and profits you want.

PROTECTING YOURSELF

The billion dollar Yellow Pages industry plots to increase revenues, leaving you, the advertiser, in the wreckage. To review, the main ways you are victimized include:

Additional directories. The profusion of new directories spreads your advertising dollar thinner without providing you with a single additional customer.

Rate increases. The industry gets you through raising their rates year after year. If you buy less, you may lose your competitive edge. Since you cannot know for certain what your competitors are up to, you have to measure the increased rates against the potential loss if you reduce your advertising program and they increase theirs. The best way to fight this is to fine tune your knowledge about how Yellow Pages advertising works, increasing your profits to cover rate increases. Look through chapters two and three of this book—the answers are there for you.

New items. Where the Yellow Pages have saturated a market, new items are introduced to bolster directory revenues. Red ink, which increases the cost of your ad by approximately 50 percent, is just one example. Clipout coupons, which present your customers with discount opportunities, appear at the back of some directories. Naturally, they up your monthly rate considerably. Super bold white pages listings is yet another new item. Finally, the color process which allows not only red but other colors to be used in Yellow Pages advertising is now being initiated.

Increased columns per page. With more columns per page, your ad gets less space but competes with a greater number of ads. Profits for the Yellow Pages increase, however, as they can fit more advertising on each page while their cost per page remains essentially the same.

Larger ads: The biggest stick-it-to-you of all, however, is offering a larger Display ad than any currently for sale. This results in increased revenues for the Yellow Pages, but it plays havoc with positioning at a heading. If you do not buy the new, larger ad, you lose your position since you must own the largest ad to ensure that newcomers to your heading are positioned behind you. All the years spent preserving your position are wasted unless you continue to play the game. For buyers of smaller Display ads, there is still a loss of position as new advertisers leap on the opportunity to cut in at the front of the line by purchasing the new, larger ad.

YELLOW PAGES SALESPEOPLE—A SPECIAL BREED

Warning: What you are about to read may sour you on the thought of meeting up with a representative of the Yellow Pages industry. Keep in mind that *not all Yellow Pages salespeople are like those described here.* But many are. When you meet one, you can decide for yourself just how closely the following descriptions apply. In the meantime, keep in mind that like going to the dentist, sometimes an unpleasant means to a necessary end is worth bearing. The profit potential of the Yellow Pages proven by businesses everywhere should serve to soften your ordeal.

Just like the industry they represent, many Yellow Pages salespeople are also looking to take a shot at you. While the average business is approached by no fewer than 25 salespeople on any day, most agree that Yellow Pages salespeople are indeed a special breed.

As an advertiser, your goal is to profit. A salesperson also wants to profit. The problem is that some salespeople focus only on what *they* stand to gain. A good salesperson will match your needs to hers, concentrating on developing a program that will do well for both of you. Others care only about how much you spend, and not whether those dollars are put where they will do you the most good.

Some Yellow Pages salespeople have been compared to pitbull dogs. It is rumored that a rather gruesome method is used to breed these animals. Two dogs are thrown into a ring to fight. When one sinks his teeth into the other, someone approaches from behind one of the dogs and, with a machete, chops off one of its hind legs. If the dog loses his grip, he is literally out of the running. If he holds his grip after being reduced to three legs, he is destined to be bred. While the truth of this story is uncertain, it is true that some of the most successful Yellow Pages salespeople are of the pitbull breed.

Salespeople converge upon the Yellow Pages industry from all types of sales backgrounds, lured by the promise of big money. No matter where they've come from, most salespeople in the industry seem to agree that selling Yellow Pages is the most challenging of all types of sales. Those that make it and survive have very special skills and talents that set them apart from their brethren who are selling other commodities. In particular, it is *tenacity* and *persistence* that mark them.

Sometimes this tenacity is born from their experiences. They know how much money can be made from Yellow Pages advertising because day after day they see it with their own eyes. If you would only allow them to show you how to do it! Other times this persistence arises from greed, with little concern about you or your needs.

Aspiring Yellow Pages salespeople spend anywhere from one to six weeks in a classroom, depending upon the company they go to work for, before ever setting foot on a customer's premises. This is necessary because just as business people find the ins and outs of the Yellow Pages overwhelming, a tremendous amount of information must be absorbed by those who represent them.

In addition to learning about Creative and Directive advertising, the Customer Circuit, the structure of the Yellow Pages, the various types of listings and ads, how to fill out contracts, why people buy and use Yellow Pages, how to describe, characterize and identify all types of listings and ads, how to construct effective ads, complete copysheets, collect from delinquent customers, the legal aspects of Yellow Pages, production and publishing, special characteristics of their product compared to the competition, and general product knowledge, the future Yellow Pagist must spend untold hours learning how to research and prepare to meet with thousands of business owners, most of whose businesses they initially know nothing about.

A Yellow Pages salesperson in training is taught to look for sales opportunities. She learns the three ways to increase a sale—a larger ad, additional headings, and selling outlying directories. She is trained to assess competition at your headings in order to learn your buying potential. She learns to use a planning guide to organize all her information. Then she is given a boatload of visual pieces to digest and trained on how to use them to sell you.

She is coached on preparing your account. She goes through many role playing exercises and is critiqued by an expert. She is taught in detail the steps of the sales presentation, from introducing herself to getting your signature on a contract.

She is also instructed on how to use interest-creating remarks to hold your attention once she gets in the door, how to dress, do's and don'ts, when to drop in on you (cold calling) and when to use the telephone for an appointment, how to get an appointment, how to get through your secretary to you, how to keep your attention once she is with you, how to arouse interest, how to fact find and learn your hot buttons, how to transition to her recommendations, words to avoid using and words to stress. She is briefed on all possible objections and how to overcome them and finally learns how to employ sales closes proven particularly successful in Yellow Pages sales.

She is taught how to work her accounts efficiently and how to manage her time. And she is tutored on methods for keeping a P.M.A. (positive mental attitude), because she will need it. Yellow Pages sales has a very high rejection rate, despite the fact that it drives many businesses.

She is then sent to ride with experienced salespeople and observe them for at least a week. Only after this is she given her territory, often a poor lot, on which to practice her new trade. Finally, she is permitted to call on businesses by herself. *(Her first call may be on your business, where she asks you to part with thousands of dollars on the basis of her recommendations!)*

Aside from being new or inexperienced, time does not permit most Yellow Pages salespeople to act as your consultants. The pressures under which they operate would make many people crack. Some sales managers, themselves under gruelling pressures from above, verbally beat their salespeople on the head to produce. If they don't produce, their jobs are on the line.

All Yellow Pages salespeople have quotas to meet. In the offices where they work, large charts are posted on the walls for the world to see, detailing how much each salesperson has sold today, this week, this canvass, and this year. If they sell nothing today, tomorrow they will get a "goose egg" (a zero) on the chart—again for the world to see.

Prizes are given to those who achieve the highest sales. Frequently, promotions are dependent upon high sales. Given these pressures, it is little wonder that most salespeople have little interest in spending their time educating you and more often are simply anxious to wrap you up and get on to the next sale.

Yellow Pages salespeople work on a variety of commissioned pay plans. One such—the net play plan—dictates that if a salesperson fails to renew an account that is currently billing $500 per month, she must now sell $500 of new monthly advertising to replace it, just to break even! But whatever the pay plan, it is designed to increase the odds that a salesperson is motivated to produce.

At some companies, additional accounts are not given to her until her numbers look good for those she has already been assigned. Instead, additional territory is sometimes the reward for high sales. With all this pressure to produce, time is the most precious commodity that the Yellow Pages salesperson has. Is it a surprise that her major concern is to make a quick sale?

It should now be clear why Yellow Pages salespeople are not the best source of objective answers to your questions. If you are a small advertiser, you now know why you are not getting the time you want; unless there is potential for you to buy and buy big, you should not be surprised to be given short shrift.

The pressures on Yellow Pages salespeople have caused them to steal territory from locked offices and "accidentally" to sell in other salespeople's protected territories. More than a few have engaged in "hanging paper," which is forging signatures or fabricating mythical businesses to whom large orders are then "sold."

Some directory companies send confirmation letters to customers who have placed orders, not so much to verify the accuracy of the order, but to catch salespeople who have created an order where none exists. *If you place an order for advertising and receive a confirmation letter, go over it carefully.* The order may have been modified after you signed it. *If you have not placed an order for advertising and receive a confirmation letter, call the company at once to advise them.*

Of course, not all salespeople respond to this situation with extreme behavior. In fact, there are many honorable and hardworking people who sell Yellow Pages for a living. But the advertising public's general impression of Yellow Pages salespeople is that they are rude and pushy and will not give you the time or service you deserve. More than any other group of salespeople, they have the reputation of lying, cheating, exaggerating or misleading.

THE BLACK SHEEP OF YELLOW PAGES SALESPEOPLE

Among Yellow Pages salespeople, those representing independent companies are often considered the black sheep. Whether a directory is published by a telephone company affiliate or by an independent has little bearing on you or the consumer. Both directories can make a profit for you and help the consumer to find what he wants. It is the salespeople representing these companies who really feel the difference.

Representatives of telephone company affiliated directories get warm receptions compared to those received by independent Yellow Pages salespeople. And fewer complaints. Whatever the facts, advertisers complain to independent directory company salespeople that their directories aren't distributed. Salespeople also take flack because their directory is missing listings. And advertisers are often reluctant to renew their ads because they found themselves alone or among only a few ads at a heading the year before. The directory's usage is hurt, they say, because consumers prefer many ads to choose from. In part, they may be right. On the other hand, for consumers who don't care, why ask for competition where you have none?

As the underdog, continually fighting the establishment Yellow Pages, independent directory salespeople are engaged in an uphill battle. Day after day of rejection and resistance takes its toll. Salespeople representing the independent companies become more aggressive and wily simply because they must to survive.

SAME TIME NEXT YEAR?

A note of consolation. If you don't like your salesperson this year, chances are you will not be seeing her again next year. Most business owners assume they see different salespeople year after year because of high turnover. In fact, that is only partially responsible.

It is the method used to distribute accounts that is really at fault. To play fair, accounts are usually assigned to salespeople randomly according to the dollar amounts spent by advertisers. For this reason, you are unlikely to see the same salesperson twice.

On the other hand, if you are happy with your salesperson and try to arrange for her to handle your account on a regular basis, for the same reasons you will probably be unsuccessful.

TRICKS OF THE TRADE

INDUSTRY JOKE

Question: *How do you tell when a Yellow Pages salesman is lying?*

Answer: *His lips are moving.*

There are a variety of ways in which Yellow Pages salespeople attempt to mislead you or to misrepresent themselves or their product. If you are not prepared and on guard, you can easily become a victim of their pranks. Following are some of the more common methods they employ.

Exaggerated Claims. Beware of outlandish promises about the returns you can expect on the dollars you invest. While a well-planned program will return a nice profit, your salesperson may imply you will get rich overnight, perceiving this as the quickest route to closing her sale. Use your common sense, and don't be carried away by dreams or fantasies.

Vague Rate Quotes. Salespeople are often deliberately vague about what the rate they quote represents. *Be aware that Yellow Pages advertising rates are quoted on a monthly, not an annual, basis.* Some less than honest salespeople count on the advertiser failing to read the contract, which states both the monthly and annual charges.

Which Yellow Pages? Salespeople who represent independent directories dread this question. It usually is asked by the experienced advertiser who is biased toward directories affiliated with the telephone company. For obvious reasons, salespeople representing independent directory companies tend to respond to this question vaguely.

You have a right to know what company you are dealing with. Be alert to an answer that is less than direct and ask to see a business card. This will establish what company the salesper - son is representing.

Directory Close Dates. Salespeople will often mislead you or even lie outright about the date a directory closes in order to get you to sign the contract before you are inclined to. Yet sometimes you have legitimate reasons for not signing immediately. You may be too busy at the moment or have to consult with an absent partner or a spouse. You might be planning to sell or to move your business or be waiting for delivery of a new logo that you want to include in your ad. You may simply need time to think things over.

Because salespeople want to close a sale as soon as possible, you may hear that the directory closes to orders this Friday, or that it is open for another month but that *she* is leaving the area on Friday. She may hint at being too busy to return later to take your order (HAH!), hoping to frighten you into signing immediately.

If you suspect you are being lied to, you can determine the actual closing date of a directory by calling the company's main office, telling them you are opening a new business, and asking them the last possible date to place an order. Since a commission is not resting on their answer, you can expect an honest one. You will now know the correct closing data (as well as something about your salesperson).

Have Mercy. The salesperson may throw herself on your mercy, claiming she will not receive more accounts until she completes what she has already been given (often the truth) or that the boss will fire her if she does not bring in your order (sometimes the truth). Whatever the ploy, it is important that you not rush into anything.

Call your salesperson's bluff by telling her that if she must have the order today, you will have to pass until next year. *Watch how fast the closing date is extended!* In fact, directory companies often deliberately leave closing dates flexible so that they can be extended during the sales campaign, if necessary.

Product Comparisons. During the course of the sales presentation, salespeople may compare the qualities and characteristics of their product or service with those of the competition. These comparisons can be inaccurate or misleading. Check these claims with the competition, or ask to see something in writing that supports them.

Getting an Appointment. The initial goal that salespeople have is to sit down with you and make their presentation. If they can't get to see you, they obviously have no hope of making a sale. For this reason, they will try a variety of ruses to get an appointment, even if you have indicated, either through your secretary or to them directly on the telephone, that you are not interested. Following are some of these ploys and ways to deal with them.

"I need to see you to verify your free listings or to update your headings." All of this can be handled on the telephone. Insist upon it if you really do not want to see her.

"I have a gift for you." Leave it at the front desk, thank you very much.

"It's not about advertising. I have a toothache and need to see you." You are a dentist. It is up to you whether you need the business badly enough to engage in this charade.

There are some unusual gimmicks salespeople use in an effort to see a reluctant prospect. As a last resort, one saleswoman pretends to be delivering a singing telegram.

Or there's the clever ploy used by a salesman I'll call Bill Green. He marches into a business and confidently introduces himself to the owner, "Hi—I'm Dorothy Green's son, Bill." The poor business owner usually assumes she's someone he should know and is too embarrassed to ask who she is. A week later the business owner is still trying to recall Dorothy Green while Bill has pocketed the fruits of that salescall.

Since all Yellow Pages directories are potentially profitable for you, it is not necessarily a waste of your time to spend a few minutes with their representatives. Besides, salespeople are notoriously easy marks for other salespeople. If you put on your selling shoes, you may be able to convert them to customers.

DECEPTIVE PRACTICES USING SURVEYS AND TESTIMONIALS

Any Yellow Pages salesperson can produce a survey that shows his directory is used more often than others. Obviously, no salesperson will show you a survey whose results are contrary to what you must believe in order to buy his product. Yet all Yellow Pages salespeople have these surveys. How is this possible?

One of the cornerstones of scientific research is the random (unbiased) sample. In order for data collected from a small group to be generalized to a larger group, the sample must reflect the larger group.

For example, if you wanted to find out which ice-cream flavor was most popular, you could telephone people at random, and if they liked ice-cream, ask them which of three flavors they preferred. If 50 of 100 people turned out to be ice-cream lovers, and 40 preferred chocolate, you could conclude that (1) half the population loves ice-cream and (2) of that ice-cream loving group, 80 percent prefer chocolate over vanilla and strawberry. *It is only possible to draw these conclusions because your sample was formed randomly.*

It would bias your sample if you only asked people who emerged from an ice-cream parlor eating chocolate ice-cream. It would be easy to predict in advance what the results of the survey would be.

I witnessed firsthand how data can be manipulated to "prove" things that simply are not true when a Yellow Pages company I worked for commissioned an "independent" research company to conduct a usage survey for them.

Researchers attempted to find out what percentage of people used each of four competing directories in an area. While they called people randomly, they made it a condition of participation in the survey that the people had this Yellow Pages company's directory in their homes. This biased the sample. People who had that directory in their home liked it and used it; people who did not have it probably did not like it and certainly could not use it. *And yet these facts were eliminated from the survey data.*

As expected, the results showed this directory received 54 percent usage in the study area. However, only half the homes called had this directory and could qualify to participate in the survey. Had everyone been included, the real figure would have been only 27 percent.

In choosing a directory to advertise in, discount surveys. And don't be swayed by testimonials either, without first checking up on them. There is a testimonial to fit every situation that a salesperson is liable to encounter. At the appropriate moment, he will produce the letters that parallel your situation and are most likely to help him to overcome your objections.

Many advertisers believe that testimonial letters are fabricated, but here are the facts. Occasionally an advertiser will send a letter to a directory company because he has been overwhelmed by helpful service, an attractive ad, or particularly good results. For the most part, however, these letters are solicited, and a token amount, such as $1, is paid for each.

Sometimes a salesperson has an extremely good rapport with a customer and asks him for a testimonial. Other times a customer offhandedly mentions that his ad did well, and the salesperson will ask him to put this information in print. In most cases, testimonials are accurate to this degree: the advertiser honestly *believes* what he is saying. The flaw is that beliefs are not facts.

Before being swayed by testimonial letters, call the business owners who provided them. You would be shocked to know how many are from businesses that are no longer around or who have changed their minds about the directory. Even if it is a valid testimonial, find out from the business owner the basis on which he makes his claims. In most cases, you will learn they are founded on perceptions, not on facts.

And a word of advice. Don't give a testimonial. If you do, you can be sure that salespeople will show it to all your competitors in an attempt to persuade them to advertise. Why be joined by them and be reduced to getting a smaller piece of the pie?

All directory companies have an ample supply of testimonial letters. This is only evidence that all directories are perceived by some to work well.

USING DIRECTORY SIZE OR GROWTH AS A SIGN OF USAGE

Even though they know better, Yellow Pages salespeople will try to convince you that the decrease in pages in their competitor's directory or the increase in theirs is related to usage. Size or growth of a directory is not a reliable method for determining how much a directory is used.

It might at first seem logical that the sheer size of a directory or the number of pages it increased or decreased over prior years would indicate its usage. After all, satisfied advertisers would renew their ads, causing a directory to grow, while unhappy advertisers would drop out, causing it to lose pages.

Unfortunately, there are many ways to "beef up" the size of a directory or reasons why it might shrink in size, none of which necessarily relates to how much it is used.

A directory can grow by leaps if the number of columns is reduced, resulting in more pages necessary to accommodate advertising. By the same token, a directory can shrink if the number of columns is increased. The number of listings in a directory may change, and this will affect its size.

Some directory companies that hurt for business because of competition may decide to give its ads away for next to nothing in order that its directory not lose pages, since they know that customers will mistakenly regard the loss as a sign of failure. For example, an independent directory company responded to a new and aggressive competitor by printing the prior year's ads, even when customers did not renew them! This maintained the size of the directory, but said nothing about its usage.

A company may decide to do a collection cleanout, severing its relationships with no-pays or slow-pays and eliminating their advertising. The directory can then lose hundreds of pages only because of a change in credit policy. Again, this says nothing about the usage of that directory.

Don't fall for false claims made by your salesperson about usage based on the size of a directory or its growth or decline.

SCARE TACTICS

In addition to the various ways that Yellow Pages salespeople try to trick you, there is also a host of ways they attempt to scare you into acting quickly.

Positioning. The fear motivator salespeople use most to get you to act right away is the effect that not acting immediately will have on the position of your ad.

If you are a current advertiser, salespeople will imply that you must act right away to preserve your position. This is not true. Once you have a seniority date, no matter when you renew your advertising, your position will not be affected. Current advertisers always take precedence over new advertisers.

If you are a new advertiser, however, it's different. With each passing day, more and more advertisers are signing up. To delay placing your order is definitely to lose ground. While it is still unwise to sign a contract on your salesperson's first visit, if you plan to advertise, make your decision as soon as possible and then act on it right away.

Your Competition. Salespeople may try to increase your sense of urgency by hinting at your competition's big advertising plans. The fact is that while your salesperson may be able to find out what your competitors are up to, why should you believe what he tells you? Even if he lies, you are still responsible for paying the bill.

This ploy is best illustrated by the situation of Joan Rosen, an attorney who would only advertise if her rival would be in the directory. Joan's salesperson agreed to find out. He later recontacted Joan, saying that her competitor would be in the directory, and Joan hurried to place her order.

In fact, the salesperson was telling the truth—Joan's rival would be in the directory—but since she had declined to advertise, she would only have a regular listing that every business in the area was entitled to at no charge. The salesperson's deceit cost Joan approximately $4,000. While she undoubtedly benefited from her ads in the Yellow Pages, as attorneys do, that is hardly the point.

Be wary of any salesperson who lets you in on your competitor's advertising plans. She may be lying. But even if she is telling the truth, how can you trust her not to tell your competition what your advertising plans are? This is highly unethical, not to mention unfair, and generally frowned upon by reputable salespeople.

Fear Itself. Aside from the profit and pride motives, fear often prompts people to buy. Salespeople know that fear of loss is one of their strongest sales tools, and they do not hesitate to use it to persuade you to sign a contract before you are ready, to keep you from canceling or cutting back, or to get you to increase your existing advertising. Be on guard if your salesperson dwells too heavily on all the catastrophes that will befall you if you fail to follow her advice. She is probably trying to frighten you into something.

Advance Copy or Showproof. Guarantee of an advance copy (a showproof or facsimile of a Display ad sent to the advertiser for viewing before the directory goes to the printer) is another of the salesperson's pressure tools. The facts are that Incolumn advertisers do not get an advance copy, so this will not be of consequence to them. Display advertisers, however, do get one, and it is important. In your ad there may be errors—such as an incorrect telephone number or address, poorly executed illustrations, or misstated hours of business— that could adversely affect your business.

While no directory company guarantees an advance copy, normally it is sent as a courtesy, provided that you place your order in time. If it is already too late, your salesperson may not even mention this fact to you, fearing that it may deter you from advertising. Be sure to ask if you will get an advance copy and when. Note your calendar to call the company if it doesn't arrive. When it does, scrutinize it. This is your last chance to correct any errors before you are locked in for a year. If your salesperson indicates that you are placing your order too late to assure an advance copy, you may be requested to sign an acknowledgment of this fact.

CONTROL OF THE SALES CALL: HOW TO KEEP IT

The magician places the cards on the table and then divides them into four piles. The subject is asked to select two piles. If one of the piles he selects holds "the card," the other two are eliminated. If not, the two piles he selected are eliminated. The magician then divides the remaining cards into additional piles, and the subject again chooses. This continues until only two piles of one card each remain.

The subject then chooses one. If it is not "the card," it is eliminated. If it is, the other is discarded. The magician then "magically" guesses the identity of that card which, of course, he has known all along.

From the start, the magician was leading the subject to selecting "the card," no matter what choices he made along the way.

Some Yellow Pages salespeople use a similar subterfuge to move their customers in a specific direction toward their goal. Instead of using piles of cards, however, they use the question and answer method, with the salesperson as "questioner" and the customer as "answerer." The questioner, like the magician, always controls the direction that events take.

Who gets and maintains control during the sales call is the real issue. There may be a tug of war over control because depending upon your luck of the draw, your goals and those of your salesperson may not be the same. In some cases, her only interest will be to access your wallet. Your need is always to access information.

If you are prepared, you can switch the usual roles and maintain control. If not, you will find yourself propelled in the direction that your salesperson has decided you should go. Consider the following typical questions that your salesperson might ask:

How much is your average customer worth?
Where do you get your business?
How much of your business comes over the telephone?
Who is your most profitable customer?
What other advertising do you do?
What is your most profitable line?
How much does it cost you to open your doors in the morning?

The answers to these questions are helpful to both you and your salesperson in assessing your Yellow Pages needs, and in that respect, the question/answer game is not harmful. *The danger lies in what is done with the answers.* You will apply them to constructing an advertising program whose scope and cost are justified for your business. Your salesperson will use your answers as ammunition against objections that arise. Your answers have real meaning to you but matter little to her because no matter what your answers are, she will use them to advance her argument.

To illustrate, below are fact-finding questions that produce very opposite answers but lead the salesperson to draw the same seemingly logical conclusion.

Salesperson: "What is your average customer worth?"

You: "$500."

Your salesperson will use this information if you object to the monthly rate. How can $350 per month be too costly when it only takes one customer to pay for your ad?

Salesperson: "What is your average customer worth?"

You: "$35."

She will now point out the importance of doing extensive advertising since you need such a large volume of customers to remain profitable.

Salesperson: "Do you get any business from the Westside?"

You: "Yes, I get some customers from there."

You have now confirmed that you can draw customers from that area and should be advertising there.

Salesperson: "Do you get any business from the Westside?"

You: "No, not really."

Salesperson: "Do you want to?"

You: "Of course. (If you are being honest.)

OR

You: "No, not really."

Salesperson: "I'm not surprised since you don't advertise there."

She now has her opening to sell you on advertising in that outlying directory.

Salesperson: "How much of your business comes over the telephone?

You: "Most of it does."

137

Salesperson: "Then you can benefit from a lot of Yellow Pages advertising."

Salesperson: "How much of your business comes over the telephone?"

You: "Not too much."

Salesperson: "Then you need more Yellow Pages advertising to increase your telephone business."

Salesperson: "What other advertising do you do?"

You: "None."

Salesperson: "Then you should advertise more in the Yellow Pages since it's your only source of advertising and you depend on it for your customers.

Salesperson: "What other advertising do you do?"

You: "I do some direct mail and run specials in the newspaper."

Salesperson: "Then you need to advertise in the Yellow Pages so customers you "create" through these more expensive forms of advertising don't call your competitors when they can't find you in the Yellow Pages."

The issue is not whether the above is logical, but whether it has any bearing on your particular business. No knee-jerk response can cover all situations. Whether you answer one way or another is immaterial to your salesperson since she knows how to use any answer to move you towards her goal. Only by staying in control—asking the questions you need answers to and adding these answers to the information you gathered during your preparation—can the program that results be tailored to your specific business needs.

THE OBJECTION/SOLUTION GAME

Your salesperson will now summarize what you have just told her, making it difficult for you to disagree, and then make a proposal. Should you object, well—fielding objections is her best sport.

Objections are expressions of opposition, disagreement, disapproval or dislike. At the same time, they may be camouflaged requests for more information. An objection is often unstated, and a sharp Yellow Pages salesperson will make it her business to find out what it is. More sales are lost because the salesperson never finds out what the objection is and as a result cannot answer it.

It is a waste of your time to play the objection/solution game with a Yellow Pages salesperson because, very simply, she is better at it than you are. Below is a list of the objections most commonly heard by Yellow Pages salespeople. They are presented here because I want you to know ahead of time that your salesperson has the answers to all of them. Not only that, she plays the sport all day long, everyday, and practice makes perfect.

All objections fall into four main categories:

•Yellow Pages do not work

> I'm not interested
> I never advertise
> I've tried Yellow Pages advertising before with no luck
> I used a test number last year and got no results

•Yellow Pages do not work for my business

> Everybody knows me
> All my business comes from word-of-mouth
> I have more business now than I can handle
> Other forms of advertising work better for me
> The big boys in my line don't advertise in the Yellow Pages
> All I get from the Yellow Pages are nuisance calls
> We have no competition
> My location brings in all my business
> I have salesmen in the field
> There are too many ads at the heading and mine would get lost
> My business is seasonal

> If people want me, they know how to find me
> My business is too small to compete
> My business is too large to have to advertise
> We don't do any local business

•Yellow Pages cost too much

> It costs too much to advertise
> I'm spending too much as it is
> My budget is done for the year and the money is
> allocated
> I'm already advertising in another directory
> There are too many directories out there
> I'm cutting back on expenses this year
> I'd have to advertise under too many headings
> Business is terrible; see me when it's better

•I don't trust your company

> I've talked with people and they don't use your book
> I don't think your books are delivered
> I've never heard of your company
> See me next year after your first directory comes out

A salesperson is well equipped to handle the first three classes of objections. She is prepared in advance to show you that the Yellow Pages work, that they can work for you, and that they do not cost, they pay. Most Yellow Pages salespeople will answer these objections easily, with the possible exception of those brand new to the job, because during training they are given pat answers to them. They memorize them, are tested on them, and practice them everyday. Engaging in a battle in this area is fruitless, unless you just want to kill some time.

The fourth class of objections—the company's credibility—can be a problem for a new directory company. Even then, salespeople usually have plenty of material on hand to show you who they are and how successful they will be. If a new company is asking for up front money, steer clear of it. If they fail to sell enough advertising to warrant publishing a directory, the company may fold, and you will be out your deposit. Would-be advertisers have lost hundreds of dollars in this way.

As with the question/answer game, the real point here is not whether the answers to these objections are valid. Many are. But they are prepared answers, and only what you have learned ahead of meeting with your salesperson will put you in a position to assess if her automatic responses to your questions and objections have any bearing on your unique situation. Only conclusions based on the facts of *your* business should be allowed to affect decisions about your advertising. That's why this book is so useful to you.

GRIP LOOSENERS

These objections may prove useful to you someday if a "pitbull" Yellow Pages salesperson has her teeth locked on your ankle and you want to loosen her grip. They are designed to get rid of a salesperson on a temporary basis. In most cases, if you use one of these objections and your salesperson persists, she comes out looking unreasonable.

"Sounds good to me, but I need to consult with my partner (or wife, father, manager, owner, etc.) Can you come back _____?" (Friday, January 15, etc.)

"I'm moving my business, possibly outside this area, and won't know where until _____(date). Can you get back to me?"

"I'm meeting with my accountant a week from Friday. Call me after that."

"I've ordered some new artwork and won't do anything until it arrives on _____ (date)." (Since orders cannot usually be processed without artwork, your signature is less meaningful as the salesperson will still have to wait for her commission.)

KILLER OBJECTIONS

If your goal is not just to buy time but to once and for all get rid of a Yellow Pages salesperson, try one of these objections. They will usually send her out the door with her tail between her legs.

"I'm going out of business."
"I'm retiring."
"I'm moving my business to Hawaii."
"I'm selling the business to someone who wishes to remain anonymous for the time being." (If you use this one, take the salesperson's business card and assure her you will pass it on to the new owner. It is important that you say the deal has been clinched. If you only indicate that you have put your business up for sale, your sales - person will begin to fire away with all the reasons you should still advertise.)

Of course, the best thing to do for everyone's sake is to say "No" when you mean it. But for those confronted by a salesperson who does not seem to understand that word, or for those who, for whatever reasons, have trouble saying "No" to salespeople, the above objections come in especially handy.

At this point you may be asking yourself, "Why do I even want to put up with this?" Let me again hammer home the answer: **Your outstanding potential to realize big profits from Yellow Pages advertising!**

SALESPEOPLE'S BIGGEST GRIPES ABOUT ADVERTISERS

In defense of Yellow Pages salespeople, a brief word on their customers. There are some pretty rotten apples in that barrel, too. The most common complaints that Yellow Pages salespeople have about their customers revolve around wasted time, rudeness, and lies.

(1) Business owners deliberately waste their time.

Customers think nothing of making one appointment after another with a commissioned salesperson and then standing her up. Others keep the appointment, but then leave the salesperson to cool her heels in the reception area for an hour or two. They then emerge from their inner den and apologize, saying they will not be able to squeeze her in today after all.

This is a cruel thing to do, particularly since the time your commissioned salesperson spends traveling to and from broken appointments and waiting for you is time she can never recoup. The result is a serious blow to her livelihood as well as time and energy stores.

(2) Business owners are unnecessarily rude.

Some business owners seem to take it as their right to be nasty to salespeople. Both male and female personnel have been yelled at, cursed at and even manhandled by customers. Granted, the behavior of some salespeople can make you see red, but it is quicker and easier to get rid of them by using a "grip loosener" or "killer" objection.

(3) Business owners lead them on.

Many business owners have no intentions of buying, but have difficulty saying "No" to salespeople. The result is that their behavior says "Yes" and keeps the salesperson coming back again and again, thinking she will get an order that she never does. By the time the salesperson figures this out, she has wasted a lot of valuable time.

It is not only her time that is wasted, but yours as well. If you don't intend to buy, say so up front or use an objection that quickly gets rid of salespeople.

(4) Business owners do not pay their bills.

Advertisers who have not paid their bills nor made any attempt to contact the directory company to make payment arrangements get livid when a salesperson brings up the matter. True, this is probably a defensive move on your part, but what did she do to deserve your wrath?

(5) Business owners lie.

They lie to salespeople about everything—from the fact that they are surveying their calls when they are not (salespeople check) to the rates they have been quoted by competing companies (salespeople usually know what these rates are).

Most business owners do not fall into these categories, but enough do to add to the burden that salespeople are already operating under.

THE CONTRACT: KNOW WHAT YOU ARE SIGNING!

Be aware that if you sign anything other than a copysheet, it can only be a contract. Your salesperson may refer to it as an order form, an application, or the paperwork, but it is definitely a contract.

Some salespeople will attempt to fool you into signing a contract before you are ready to by implying you are only signing to reserve space or to secure a position or to get the ball rolling on the artwork. Nothing could be farther from the truth! Only a signed contract reserves space or a position. Preliminary artwork can be done for you without a signed contract. Only the final artwork, which is done by the publisher, is prepared on the basis of a signed contract.

READING TERMS BEFORE YOU SIGN

It is surprising how few people take the time to read a contract before signing it. Contracts for Yellow Pages advertising, often in amounts equal to that necessary to purchase a new automobile, are casually signed. Few bother to turn it over and read the terms.

The terms of an average contract for Yellow Pages advertising spell out, among other things, that:

(1) Your position is not guaranteed. (Did your salesperson imply what position you would have, how good it would be, or where on the page your ad would appear?)

(2) Any claims for damages do not exceed the total amount of the advertising. (There is no price that can be put on what it would cost you if an incorrect telephone number were to appear in your ad, or the ad itself were omitted.)

(3) The directory can be long-lifed (extended) from its normal 12 month existence to as many as 18 months. (And you are obligated to pay for it.)

(4) Late charges accompany late payments, and the entire balance may become due immediately, including interest, if even one payment is late.

(5) You pay all costs and fees in the event of any legal action against you.

(6) Your obligation to pay does not cease if you sell your business or go out of business unless certain requirements are met.

(7) There are conditions for cancellation.

Frequent problems and misunderstandings arise over all these matters because people do not take the time to read the terms of this legal, binding contract.

WHAT YOU SHOULD GET BEFORE YOUR SALESPERSON LEAVES

You have signed a contract for directory advertising (hopefully after reading its terms), and the salesperson is packing up and making ready to depart. Before she leaves, make sure that you have taken the following steps:

1) Verify information and get a copy of the contract. If it has not been done, go over the contract with her to make sure that your name, address and telephone number are correct. Verify the directories you have bought space in, the ad sizes you have chosen, and the headings under which the ads will appear. Note the monthly and annual totals in their appropriate boxes on the contract. *And get a copy of the contract.* Only if you have a copy are you protected if the salesperson modifies it after leaving you, if your telephone number is printed incorrectly, if the ad size is incorrect, etc.

2) Identifying Information. Get your salesperson's business card. It should clearly indicate her name, a telephone number where she can be reached, and the name, address and telephone number of the company she represents. Also get the name and telephone number of her manager. If she resigns, you must know this if you need to have any further dealings with the company.

3) Copies of the Copysheets. If ad copy is involved, get copies of the copysheets. This is the only way you can protect yourself should she change anything in your ad after leaving you. This is particularly important in the case of

Incolumn ads as you will not receive an advance copy to check for mistakes or changes.

4) Directory Closing Date. Ask her to write down the date the directory closes and to affix her signature to it. If you want to make any changes in your advertising later, you must know the final date to do so.

5) Cancellation Policy. Cancellation procedures are not normally brought up by either you or the salesperson at the time of the sale. Later, however, they may take on great importance. You might change your mind about advertising—whether it be because of buyer's remorse, a decision to close or move your business, a new partner's objections, a better opportunity with another Yellow Pages company, or simply a desire to reduce the amount of advertising you ordered.

Ask your salesperson the terms under which you may cancel, and have her point out where on the contract that policy is described. If cancellation is allowed, there is usually a final date to do so that appears on the contract. (If cancellation is not permitted, you might want to think twice about advertising with this company.)

In the case where it is permitted, find out whether a telephone call is sufficient or if you must cancel in writing, a better idea in any case. The best idea is to send the letter registered with a return receipt requested to show that your letter was received and who received it. The cost of a letter sent this way is nominal, and it could save you a great deal later. Commissioned salespeople are not keen on having orders cancelled after investing a lot of time and effort in securing them. A telephone request or unregistered letter asking for cancellation has a funny way of being ignored by a commissioned salesperson.

Only after you have taken the above steps should you permit the salesperson to leave. You can then rest assured that you have done everything possible to protect yourself in the event you want to make changes in your program, to cancel your advertising, or to get an adjustment if there is an error.

GETTING ADJUSTMENTS FOR ERRORS

Despite all your best efforts and those of the many people who will handle your order before the directory is published, errors are made. Many of them are directly traceable to carelessness on your part in verifying information. Others result from lack of experience or haste on the part of the salesperson. Some errors, however, are made by the directory company's production department or by the publisher.

Errors of many types can be made, including incorrect or omitted information, poor illustrations, or ads placed at incorrect headings. If you follow the above instructions and become the victim of an error, you have a good chance to get an adjustment.

Normally adjustments are made by crediting your account with an amount judged to cover your inconvenience or potential lost business resulting from the error. Sometimes a 100 percent adjustment is made if it is believed that you were greatly wronged by the error. An incorrect telephone number usually warrants a complete adjustment. But as spelled out in the terms of the contract, *in no case can you expect to collect anything in excess of the total amount of your advertising bill.*

How much a 100 percent adjustment fails to compensate an advertiser for an error is illustrated by a case where a bold listing under a national manufacturer was inadvertently omitted by a directory company for an authorized television repair center. Researching their past invoices, the business estimated that as much as $6,000 was lost as a result of the omitted listing. The total cost of the listing, however, was $72, and that was the total adjustment they received—according to the terms of the contract.

Squeak Loudly. If an error is not your fault, the old adage—the squeakiest wheel gets the most oil—definitely applies. Most directory companies have customer service departments that investigate your complaint and then decide how large an adjustment will be made. They are much more responsive to customers who persist loudly. Not surprisingly, the most generous adjustments are usually given to businesses that continue to advertise and to those that spend the most advertising dollars.

Rally Support. To get the largest possible adjustment in the event of an error, have your salesperson and her manager go

147

to bat for you. Customer service workers are very company oriented. Further, they deal with complaining customers day in and day out and develop a somewhat cynical and calloused attitude towards them. On the other hand, your salesperson and her manager are more interested in seeing you satisfied since their future incomes are dependent upon how happy you and other wronged customers are made. While there are no guarantees that this will produce better results, it will give you a better shot.

CHANGING YOUR PROGRAM AFTER PLACING YOUR ORDER

After you have signed a contract for advertising, you may decide that you want to change what you ordered. It may be a simple change, such as adding a newly acquired telephone number to your Display ad or replacing your logo with an updated one. Since placing your order you may have added a new line of products that you want to bring to the public's attention. Perhaps you eliminated a service and want to delete all ad copy that refers to it. Whatever the change, be sure to notify the directory company in writing, asking them to send your salesperson out to handle it.

The reason for this is that as far as your salesperson is concerned, you are now a closed book. She leads a very pressured work life, and her attention and time is much more likely to be given to a sale in the making rather than to yesterday's news. Go on record with the company as requesting a change rather than waiting for your salesperson to respond to your telephone call or to drop by at her convenience. If you want to cancel your advertising altogether, it is all the more important that you advise the company in writing as soon as possible with a registered letter, return receipt requested.

IF YOU SELL YOUR BUSINESS

Even if you decide to sell your business, it may not be a bad idea to continue advertising. Businesses often do not sell as quickly as expected, and your ledgers will look better to a potential buyer if you keep your sales up. You may also be glad to have that advertising next year if you still own the business.

If you sell your business before the contract with the directory company expires, you can spell out in the escrow papers that the new owner is to assume the payments since he will be the one benefiting from any business the ads draw. He may even be glad to have an on-going advertising program. If he does not want it, however, you, and not he, will be liable for the bill since you signed the contract.

IF YOU GO OUT OF BUSINESS

If the property rather than the business is being sold and a different type business goes in, then the advertising will not benefit anyone. In this case, you will likely be considered "out of business" and relieved of the obligation to pay the bill. This is provided you have met the conditions of the contract and simply not moved your business to a nearby location, retaining your old telephone number or adding a referral to a new number.

Forgiving advertising debts owed by an "out of business" is not merely goodwill on the part of the directory company. It is also good sense. Taking you to court, where they will have a difficult time proving that you are benefiting from the advertising, is not worth their while. If you legitimately go out of business, in most cases your obligation to pay the bill ceases. Some companies will forgive advertising debts to advertisers who keep the same telephone number but change the nature of their business to a degree that the advertising clearly no longer benefits them, such as a plumber who becomes a locksmith.

IF YOU CHANGE YOUR LOCATION

If you move your business but keep the same telephone number or put a referral on it to your new number, you are still obligated to continue to pay for the advertising since you will still be benefiting from telephone calls. Only completely disconnecting the line with no referral will generally release you from this obligation.

IF YOU DISCONNECT YOUR TELEPHONE

Some businesses, dissatisfied with results from their Yellow Pages advertising, disconnect the telephone number that is displayed in their ads. Sometimes they plan to do this from the start, so they purposely put a telephone number in their ads that, if disconnected, will not hurt them.

Even if they continue to do business at the same address, a directory company's attempts to collect are rarely successful. The legal test seems to be degree of benefit. Since the Yellow Pages is so tied to the telephone, when a caller reaches a disconnected number, it is unlikely she will follow up with a visit to the business's premises.

WARNINGS TO NEW ADVERTISERS

As a new advertiser, you are particularly vulnerable to the Yellow Pages advertising force. Perhaps you are starting a new business. Or you may have been in business for a while but are changing its thrust from wholesale to retail and need advertising. Or you have simply not seen fit to advertise in the Yellow Pages before.

The vulnerability of a new advertiser stems from a lack of experience. While experience alone does not exempt you from being taken by a dishonest salesperson or from failing to optimize your money-making potential, a lack of it leaves you defenseless.

New businesses are particularly in need of Yellow Pages as they must quickly become grounded or join the 50 percent of new businesses that fail during their first year of operation. (For some types of businesses, the statistic is even higher—90 percent of restaurants go under before the first year is up.) Because of their increased need, people new to Yellow Pages advertising are often taken advantage of. For this reason, they must be on the alert and as informed as possible.

As mentioned before, new advertisers often mistake the monthly rate for the annual rate. It happens frequently enough that it is worth repeating. *Make sure you understand that rates are quoted on a monthly basis.* You must multiply that figure by 12 to get your annual total. New advertisers are also less aware of the great number of directories they have to choose among to cover their market. They sign up for Yellow Pages advertising and are startled when a salesperson representing a different directory company shows up the next day.

Often they leave too many decisions to the salesperson, whether related to ad copy, ad size, or which directories to advertise in. Your salesperson, of course, will be more than happy to make all your decisions for you, but they may turn out to be in her best interests rather than in yours. **Read this book thoroughly and follow all the guidelines before meeting with anyone from the Yellow Pages.**

WARNINGS TO CONTINUING ADVERTISERS

Current advertisers who survey their Yellow Pages respon - ses during the year are in an excellent position to render profit- making decisions about next year's program. Unfortunately, informed advertisers represent a fraction of their group.

For most, it will once again be a guessing game. Your salesperson, on the other hand, will come to your door, certain of what you should do and fully prepared to renew your advertising with an eye to increasing it. She will also be fit to do battle with you if you want to decrease or cancel it.

Yellow Pages salespeople know from experience that what advertisers say to them initially has little bearing on the final outcome. They expect that most advertisers will want to leave their advertising the same, cut back, or cancel altogether. Because the opinions of advertisers are usually not based on reliable data, they have little confidence in their decisions and are easily swayed by the claims of salespeople, testimonial letters from other advertisers (who they believe surveyed their customers for results), and company surveys that "prove" the directory is being used.

You should not allow your emotions to guide you or make your decisions on the basis of what your salesperson tells you. You must be informed if you are not to fall into the category of the easily swayed advertiser. Base your decisions on data from last year's advertising and follow the steps and rules in this book.

DON'T SAY "LEAVE IT THE SAME"

Occasionally advertisers want to increase their advertising. Sometimes they want to cut back or cancel completely. But by far the response that Yellow Pages salespeople are greeted with most often is, "Leave it the same." This is usually based less on satisfaction with advertising results as it is on the fact that no thought has been given to it during the year.

Because you are contacted by the Yellow Pages only once a year, you have just this one opportunity to update your advertising. Changes should be made based on last year's results and on the the knowledge you've gained from reading this book. You may find there are areas where you need to decrease your advertising. You may also find areas where you are under-advertised. Keep in mind that advertising is not a fixed expense in the way that rent is. It is an investment, with the potential for a big payoff.

You must also alter your ad copy to reflect changes that have occurred in your business during the year or that you plan to make in the near future. Remember, on the basis of what is in your ad, you hope to draw enough customers for a full year to keep your business profitable.

Any salesperson worth her salt disregards the remark "Leave it the same," whether from concern for you or because accepting it runs counter to her hopes of increasing your advertising. But a salesperson who is too tired to argue, or inexperienced and just grateful not to take a loss, may accept your decision. *This is a potential disaster for you.* As much as the new advertiser must be on guard from lack of experience, it is just as important that you be, too. Look again at the section in Chapter Three on updating your advertising, pages 116-117.

Chapter Five

CHECKING
ON HOW YOUR
ADVERTISING
IS WORKING

MONITORING AD RESULTS

Once your Yellow Pages program is in place, the next step is to find out how it works. There are several methods you can use to monitor how many customers you get and how much they spend.

Most of you intend to stay in business. The Yellow Pages, too, seems to be here to stay. This means that unless you make the effort to track your advertising results this year, you are victimizing yourself. The best you can hope for next year is to continue with the hit and miss approach, likely following one bad investment with another. Year after year you will be plagued by the Yellow Pages, unsure if your investment is paying off, and unable to know how to change your program so that it will.

Experience has shown me that once business owners sign up for Yellow Pages advertising, they tend to forget about it. From then on, they pay little or no attention to finding out what works and how well. As a result, when they are contacted by the Yellow Pages the next year, decisions are made strictly on the basis of impressions. Ads are renewed, cancelled, or changed in a haphazard manner. This is a strange way to treat an investment.

Worth Remembering

*Don't wait for customers to tell you
they found you in the Yellow Pages.
Ask them.*

WHY THERE IS LITTLE RELIABLE YELLOW PAGES DATA

Because of this, there aren't many solid facts about which directories, ads or headings work best. In cases where advertisers have tried to monitor their Yellow Pages results, the information is often unreliable. Blessed be those few who keep accurate records that produce solid data and provide the little reliable information available.

It is not that you have no interest in getting the answers to these questions, but that it is difficult to do. In most cases, you are too busy or your employees, who have the most contact with customers, are uncooperative or can't be depended upon. In some cases, you simply forget. In no other instance do people continue to make large yearly investments without factual information about how such investments have fared in the past. Would you put money into a savings accounts without knowing the rate of interest it paid? Yet that is what most of you do with the dollars you invest in the Yellow Pages.

Thousands of advertisers, persuaded by Yellow Pages salespeople to monitor their calls, have been shocked to find how off their perceptions and beliefs are about what is or is not working for them. Track the results of your advertising so that in future years you will know how to increase your profits by using the Yellow Pages. Here are some ways to keep track.

SURVEYING TELEPHONE SHOPPERS

A Test Number. You can install a telephone number to be used only for testing your Yellow Pages ads. It is important, of course, that this number appear only in the ads you want to test and not be circulated elsewhere. If you don't want to go to the expense of installing a separate line just for this purpose, perhaps you already have a line with an uncirculated number that you can use for your test.

Since the number will only be published in your Yellow Pages ads, when it rings you know where the call is coming from. Business resulting from the call is then directly attributable to the Yellow Pages.

RCF: THE MOST RELIABLE METHOD

The best way to use a test number in your ad is with the aid of RCF. When you have an RCF number in your ad, the telephone company sends you a monthly itemization of all calls that have come in on that number because you pay for these calls as part of your RCF program. There is no question of how many calls you have gotten because you have a written record of them.

This prevents problems that otherwise plague a test number survey. The calls must be consistently tallied as they come in. Although this seems easy enough, you are depending on your employees who can make mistakes or be busy, forgetful or lazy. If records are incomplete, inaccurate or not kept at all, only a vague impression of the number of calls is conveyed rather than an accurate count.

You can see how RCF circumvents this problem. An added advantage of using an RCF number to test an ad is that if after a few months your results are poor, you can disconnect the number and your obligation to pay the bill usually ceases.

In either case, however, unless you already have a line available to use for test purposes, you must go to the expense of installing and maintaining one. It is particularly expensive if you have to install several lines because you want to test several ads.

ROTARY LINES: THEIR UNRELIABILITY IN TESTS

Since most directory companies do not permit the use of a rotary number in an ad unless the primary number also appears, a test of this type does not produce good data. Some of the calls from your ad will come in on your primary line, but you will not know their source.

In addition, a rotary line does not give an accurate call count. Since it will also ring if the lines preceding it are busy, you have no way of knowing when it rings if the call is coming from the Yellow Pages. Using the last line of a set of rotary numbers is like having a single line. There is no backup when a customer calls and finds it busy. A customer getting a busy signal is not likely to wait, but may call someone else. This results in lost business.

Asking customers how they found you. An obvious way to find out how your Yellow Pages ads are working is to ask callers how they found you. A simple question, "How did you hear about us?" will tell you.

Sourcing by page number. Sourcing calls by page number helped Harold Fishman, a piano tuner, to fine tune his own operation. He ran small Display ads in three different directories. By asking each caller for the page number and keeping accurate records, he learned that while all three ads made the telephone ring, only one directory was bringing in calls that were followed up by requests for his services. The following year he cut back on his advertising in the two non-productive directories and kept only his successful ad. In this way he got just as much business as he had the year before, but paid considerably less for it.

You can further pinpoint the source of a call and the amount of business it generates. When a caller says he found you in the Yellow Pages, he probably has the directory in front of him and can tell you the page number he is looking at. This will tell you specifically which directory, heading or ad was responsible for the call. You can also record how many of these callers are converted to customers and how many dollars they spend. This results in specific information on the return of your invested advertising dollars.

Inserting a signifier in your ad: Some advertisers have successfully surveyed their calls by putting a letter or number in their ads and then asking callers to identify it. This can easily pinpoint the directory, heading and ad that gets the credit for the call.

Walt Glassell of Best Glass & Mirror advertises at multiple headings in many directories and includes a number in the upper right-hand corner of every ad. By asking the customer for that number under the guise of serving him faster, Walt is able to learn exactly which part of his advertising program is responsible for his business. He is thoroughly equipped to base next year's programs on real facts and put his dollars where they do most good.

Aside from numbers and letters, there are other signifiers you can use. A phrase such as "Mention this ad for a 10 percent discount" or "Ask about our monthly specials" are examples. Pete Peterson of Sunrise Auto Repair uses the signifier "Ask for Ray." Since Ray is his dog's name, hearing it is a clear indication that the Yellow Pages is working for him.

This type of signifier has the advantage of taking the burden of sourcing from you and placing it on your caller. Unfortunately, he has less at stake and may neglect to mention the signifier, whether because he forgets or is embarrassed. Since you are the one who stands to gain, it is best that you take responsibility for learning how your ads are working.

SURVEYING WALK-IN SHOPPERS

Some businesses have mostly walk-in customers. If yours falls into this category, ask customers you have not seen before how they heard about you. If they say "The Yellow Pages," make a note of the dollars they spend. This lets you know not only how many customers your ads are bringing in, but also how many dollars they are producing.

If you advertise in more than one directory and want to pinpoint which one customers used to find you, you will quickly discover that they aren't able to tell you. The majority of consumers are unaware that there are different directory companies and believe instead that the telephone company delivers all their directories to them.

To overcome this problem, tear the covers off the directories in which you advertise and keep them handy under the counter. When a customer indicates he found you in the Yellow Pages, pull out the covers and ask him to point to the one that was on the directory he used to look you up. Chances are that the correct directory will be identified.

Some business owners think that customers will be offended or annoyed if they are surveyed. On the contrary, people generally like to help others. Tell your customers that they'd be doing you a big favor by helping you to know how your advertising is working. You'll find them happy to participate.

159

The flaws inherent in the method of directly asking customers how they found you are similar to those of the test number method—when you or your employees get too busy or forget or when you do not keep accurate records of customer responses, your data is unreliable and not useful.

CUSTOMERS OVERLOOKED BY SURVEYS

Surveying customers will not always tell you when referral customers have gotten your telephone number from the Yellow Pages. Experience shows that they are more apt to say, "Mrs. Smith referred me," in the hopes of getting better service. Yet had you not been visible in the Yellow Pages, you may have lost this referral to a competitor.

It is also difficult to know how many of your referral customers were generated by a customer who originally found you in the Yellow Pages. For the past ten years I have been referring friends and acquaintances to a carpenter I found in the Yellow Pages with whom I was extremely satisfied. He probably has no idea that the Yellow Pages is indirectly responsible for them.

THE CUSTOMER SURVEY FORM

Following is a form you can use to help you keep track of where your business is coming from. Of course, you will have nothing to enter on the form if you fail to survey your customers. If your staff answers the telephone and deals with customers, instruct them on how to collect this information. *Emphasize how important it is to you.* This information is *so* valuable to you that you might even consider providing incentives to ensure that your employees cooperate. A poor return on your Yellow Pages investment is bad enough, but missing out on its rich harvest is nothing less than a shame.

Customer Survey Form

Advertising Results From _____ **to** _____

Source	Use STROKE CHECK (卌 ll) Put page # that ad appears on in box				TOTAL	PER-CENT
YELLOW PAGES _____ (Identify Directory)						
YELLOW PAGES _____ (Identify Directory)						
YELLOW PAGES _____ (Identify Directory)						
REFERRALS						
NEWSPAPER						
MAGAZINE						
DIRECT MAIL						
RADIO						
OTHER						

Find out which advertising investments are paying off!

161

STEP BY STEP TROUBLESHOOTING

Surveying your customers pinpoints your successes and failures. You are now able to know which directories work, which ads are successful and which headings are profitable. You will want to keep these ads or even increase them, if they work particularly well. Non-productive directories, ads or headings represent trouble areas because advertising should pay, not cost. These trouble areas must be examined in order to find out what the problems are and how to correct them.

Troubleshooting—finding out why and where something went wrong and how to fix it—is easily accomplished by following the procedures outlined below. They only work, of course, if your results are based on accurate records of customer activity during the year.

PROBLEM ....

Your ad has brought in calls, but at a rate of few to none.

PROCEDURE ....

(1) Check to make sure that your ads appear under the correct headings and that the telephone numbers in them are correct.

(2) Verify to the best of your ability that the directory has been distributed. Check to see if you received one. Visit the businesses on your street to see if they got theirs. Call friends or relatives that live in the directory area to determine whether they received copies. Since people are usually not aware of all the different directories and have difficulty telling them apart even when informed, have them read to you from the front cover the name of the publisher and the area the directory includes.

If the telephone number in your ad is correct, your ads appear at the correct headings, and it seems that the directory has been distributed, go on to the next step.

(3) Look at the headings where your ads appear. How does your position measure up? If you are on the 17th page of a

heading because you chose the smallest ad, you may have stumbled upon part of your problem. (You can count on your salesperson pointing this out to you next year when she arrives to renew your program.)

(4) If your position is adequate, look carefully at the page on which your ad is printed. Is your ad in the gutter? This is unfortunate, but uncontrollable, as placement on the page is never guaranteed. You can remedy this situation next year by purchasing an ad size that makes it unlikely to be guttered.

(5) If page placement does not appear to be at blame, the next step is to compare your ad with others on the page. If you lack objectivity, ask friends or employees to point out the ads on that page that catch their eye. *(Where the eye stops, the sale begins.)* Are other ads grabbing the shopper's attention first? If so, plan to revamp your artwork next year. If the consensus is that all ads draw the attention equally, proceed to the next step.

(6) Call two or three of your competitors who have ads at the heading, and ask them how their ads are working for them. It may be necessary to pose as the owner of a similar business located at a distance who has been contacted by a salesperson from that directory company and who wants to hear about it from someone who has tried it. If you reveal your true competitive identity and the directory is working, your competitors may not tell you. If it is not working, they may say it is, hoping to see you throw your money away rather than to put it to use more effectively where it might hurt them. Don't forget to ask how they know their advertising is working or not as you are interested in facts, not impressions.

(7) If your competitors indicate poor results and appear to have good data to back up their claims, the fault may lie in the general economy, about which there is little you can do. If they tell you that their ads are working well, head for the nearest mirror, look yourself in the eye, and ask: "Is my reputation for shoddy work or price gouging keeping people from calling me?" (The answer is between you and your mirror.)

PROBLEM ....

You receive calls, but they are generally nuisance calls—people wanting things you do not carry, asking for services you do not provide, or calling from areas you do not service.

PROCEDURE ...

Your ad does not accurately reflect what your business is about and does not talk to the markets you want to target. You will have to live with it this year, but plan to go back to the drawing board next year, following the steps covered earlier for designing an effective ad.

PROBLEM ...

You are receiving inquiries of substance from customers, but they are not turning into business.

PROCEDURE ...

Your ad is working well. The Yellow Pages have fulfilled their responsibility by making your telephone ring. But are you meeting yours?

WHERE THE RESPONSIBILITY OF THE YELLOW PAGES STOPS AND YOURS STARTS

Don't be surprised if your salesperson checks up on you if you claim to be sourcing your calls. After she leaves you, from time to time she may call your business and pose as a customer. If your business is a small one, where you are likely to answer the telephone and recognize her voice, she may have a male co-worker call instead. (She, of course, will return the favor for him at some future time.)

When she calls, she will ask a few questions and then make a note of the date and time of her call and, if possible, the name of the person she spoke with. Later, armed with this information, she will recontact you. If you are surveying your calls and she has integrity, she will want you to know which calls were from her so that you can eliminate that information from your data.

The reason she does this is not to get evidence with which to call you a liar, but because she has to know if the results you claim are based on surveying customers or not. If they are, she must look elsewhere to account for poor results. If they are not, she knows that you do not have any data on which to make a judgment about how your ads are working, and her job is to get you to survey your calls.

In most cases, calls are not being surveyed—either because of a lack of interest or an unwillingness to go to the trouble. Sometimes you may honestly believe your employees are sourcing customers when, in fact, they are not. If this is the case, you may genuinely be glad to know this so you can get after them about it. If they are not sourcing calls and yet providing you with sourcing information, it is probably fabricated to get you to think they are doing their job. This is far worse than their not sourcing at all since it is guaranteed to mislead you in future advertising decisions.

A by-product of your salesperson checking to see if you are sourcing your calls is that she inadvertently learns a lot about how you treat your callers. She may find your employees rude and abrupt or discourteous and unhelpful. It is not surprising that shoppers are looking elsewhere to do their business.

Some businesses are simply unprepared to provide the products or services their ads claim they do. In other cases, prices may be so out of line that it is understandable that customers end up doing business with a competitor.

The responsibility of the Yellow Pages is to make your telephone ring. Your responsibility is to sell callers on doing business with you. If you fail in your job, it is unfair to blame it on the Yellow Pages.

If your ads are making the telephone ring but not producing business, check your telephone behavior against the following standards:

1. Answer your telephone no later than the third ring. Shoppers tend to be impatient. If you let your phone ring too long before answering it, you may be greeted by a dial tone when you finally pick it up.

2. Check up on your answering service. If you must use an answering service, check its promptness in responding to your callers by telephoning *your* number (not the number you call to get your messages which the answering service knows is being called by its customers) at least once a day. Check for calls frequently and return then as soon as possible. If you delay, by the time you get back to the caller, he may already have found someone else to do business with.

3. Avoid answering machines. Although popular, the easiest way to kill your business is by having an answering machine pick up your calls. It generally presents the image of a small, kitchen-table operation. Consumers have indicated their belief that a larger business is more reliable and better suited to serve their needs. On top of this, a caller usually wants to speak to somebody right away.

If you cannot avoid using an answering machine, check for calls often and return them as soon as possible. Businesses that deal in a product or service that might be used in an emergency situation should *never* use answering machines. Envision a frantic woman, knee-deep in water, calling a plumber and finding herself talking to a machine!

Sam Garcia runs Robertson Towing, a one-man operation. He used an answering machine to pick up calls when he was out on a job. While he claimed he got poor results from his ad, he did concede that when he returned to his office and checked his machine, he often found hangups. Given the nature of his business and the prominent claim in his ad of 24 hour emergency service, he had no one to blame for his ad's poor results but himself.

4. Handle callers courteously and helpfully. The telephone company provides businesses with free booklets on telephone etiquette. Request some, and go over the material with your employees. A telephone call is the first encounter that shoppers have with your business. If you called a business and were dealt with in a rude or unhelpful manner, would you want customers, who may leave your store without making a purchase if they receive bad treatment.

5. Keep promises to callers. If you agree to meet someone at 10 a.m., be there. If for a good reason you cannot, call to let him know before he takes it upon himself to find someone else who can. If you agree to get back to a caller with information or an estimate, do so as soon as possible. If the information is not available by the time promised, call him anyway to let him know you are working on it. The number one reason someone decides to do business with you is because he likes you. Make a caller like you, and you are on your way to making a customer of him. If you are too busy to do the work right away, tell him. Stringing a customer along only angers him. If you are honest, you may not get his business now, but he will remain a potential future customer.

6. Tell callers if you do not carry the product or perform the service they need. Customers appreciate honesty, and you are not prevented from selling them another product or service that may suit their needs as well or better. Or surprise them by referring them to a competitor. Nothing will make you look better. When your competitor learns of your generosity, he may do the same for you.

7. Never run down your competitors. Consumers who were polled indicated that this was one of the main reasons they decided not do business with someone. Bad-mouthing your competition reflects more poorly on you than on your competitors.

If you are not following these suggestions, start now. You will increase the chances that calls generated by the Yellow Pages are followed up by business.

Worth Remembering

*Refer customers to your competitors
if you don't have what they need.
It makes you look good!*

AFTERWORD

You have a wealth of information if you have read all of this book from cover to cover—and the word "wealth" is used deliberately. If you put into practice what you have learned in the course of your reading, you are capable of creating a profitable Yellow Pages advertising program for your business.

A program with these elements promises you a good return on your investment in the Yellow Pages:

(1) the correct directories, headings and ad sizes for *you,*

(2) effective ads that draw the customers *you* want to attract,

(3) *your* effective sales follow-up with these customers.

Take responsibility for seeing that you have that kind of program, and you will agree that buying this book was the best money *you* ever made!

Worth Remembering

*Decisions don't come from a confused
mind...only from a clear one.*

Index

Printstyles: 50
Profits:
    determining, 155
    industry and, 20
Promotionals: 88
Proof: 135

Q

Question/answer game: 136-138

R

Random sampling: 130-131
RASCALS: 70-74
Rates:
    as affected by distribution, 40,
        84, 98
    comparative formula for, 41
    comparison of, 98
    determining of, 83-84
    increases in, 121
    judging importance of, 99
    independent vs. telephone
        company, 85-86
    negotiation of, 86-87
    varying of, 84
    vs. cost, 98
    waiving increases in, 87
Rates & Data: 40, 86
RCF: 89-90, 157
Red ink: 61-62, 121
Relocating a business: 149
Remote Call Forwarding: 89-90
    as survey technique, 157
Replacing customers: 8-10
Residential listings:
    usefulness of, 24-25
Residential numbers in ads, 75
Reverse: 60-61
Rotary numbers:
    avoiding payment with, 75-76
    tests and, 157-158

S

Salespeople:
    as a special breed, 122-126
    as biased sources of
        information, 125-126
    deceptions with testimonials,
        131-132
    deceptions with surveys,
        130-131
    dishonesty of, 126
    gripes about advertisers,
        142-143
    independent company, 126-127
    misrepresentation by, 128-130
    objection/solution game,
        138-142
    payplans of, 125
    question/answer technique,
        135-138
    reputations of, 126
    scare tactics of, 133-135
    telephone company, 127
    training of, 123-125
    tricks of, 128-130
Sampling: 130-131
Scare tactics: 133-135
Screens: 60-61
Selling a business: 148-149
Sharing of ads: 77
Showproof: 135
Signifiers: 158-159
Slogans: 71-74
Sourcing customers: 155-161
Space ads:
    vs. Display ads, 35
    vs. Listings, 34
Specialized directories: 20
Specialty Guides: 110-111
Super Bold white pages listings:
    29
Survey form: 160-161
Surveying customers: 155-161
Surveys:
    by page number, 158

by signifier in ad, 158-159
customers overlooked by, 160
directory usage and, 130-131
of telephone shoppers, 156-159
of walk-in customers, 159-160

T

Targeting customers: 46, 50, 53, 65-68
Telephone company directories:
residential numbers in, 75
usage of, 23
Tell-Tales: 27
Terms of the contract: 144-145
Test number:
as customer survey method, 156-159
Testimonial letters: 131-132
Trademark, Custom: 31
Trademarks: 31-32
Tradenames: 31-32
Tricks of the trade: 128-130
Troubleshooting:
procedures for, 162-164

U

Updating advertising:
115-116, 152
Usage:
directory growth and, 132-133
directory size and, 132-133
distribution and, 90-92
print size and, 27
Usage surveys:
distortion of, 130-131

V

Victim:
of industry, 80-81, 121-122
of salespeople, 122-139
of advertiser's mistakes, 155

W

Wagner Yellow Pages Profit
Formula, The:
components of, 98
uses of, 98-103
Walk-in shoppers:
surveying, 159-160
Walking Fingers: 23, 94
White pages: 24
White pages listings: 24-25

Y

Yellow Pages:
classified, 25